Just Write That Book Already!

How to Avoid Distractions,

Create a Writing Schedule,

and Organize your Ideas so you can get
started on your Book Today

Joy Farrington

Just Write That Book Already!
JUST WRITE THAT BOOK ALREADY!

HOW TO AVOID DISTRACTIONS, CREATE A WRITING SCHEDULE, AND ORGANIZE YOUR IDEAS SO YOU CAN GET STARTED ON YOUR BOOK TODAY

JOY FARRINGTON
JOY THE LIT DIVA

WWW.LITDIVA.COM

DEDICATION

I dedicate this book to my son. Daelon, you are my life force; you are my everything. Keep shining, and one day you will forever change the world. Sending you love and light, forever.

Testimonials

"I AM A FREQUENT USER OF (LIT DIVA INC.) SERVICES. THE DIRECT MARKETING SERVICES ARE CREATIVE, FOCUSED, timely and affordable for every tier of promotioN. JOY FARRINGTON IS PROFESSIONAL, RESPONSIVE AND A PLEASURE TO WORK WITH. I PARTICULARLY LIKE THAT SHE IS WILLING TO BE FLEXIBLE AND ACCOMMODATING TO HER CLIENTS AND THEIR WORK. I WOULD RECOMMEND HER SERVICE TO ANYONE WHO WANTS TO PROMOTE AND ADVERTISE THEIR BOOK."

CAROL TAYLOR
BESTSELLING AUTHOR OF THE BROWN SUGAR 4-BOOK FICTION SERIES AND THE EX CHRONICLES. AWARD-WINNING BOOK EDITOR, FORMERLY OF RANDOM HOUSE.

"IF YOU ARE EVER LOOKING TO MARKET YOUR BOOK ONLINE, I WOULDN'T LOOK ANYWHERE ELSE BUT TO JOY FARRINGTON! SHE WAS PROMPT, PROFESSIONAL, AND CREATIVE WITH HER IDEAS OF MARKETING MY BOOK. I AM SO GLAD I DECIDED TO USE HER!"

RYAN C. MACK
OPERATION HOPE, INC. MID-ATLANTIC MARKET PRESIDENT, CNN, FOX, & CNBC CONTRIBUTOR, AND BESTSELLER AUTHOR

JOY FARRINGTON IS A CONSUMMATE PROFESSIONAL. HER PASSION FOR LITERATURE SPILLS OVER INTO HER WORK. SHE SUPPORTS WRITERS, BOOK CLUBS, AND READERS. JOY KNOWS HOW TO BRING ESTABLISHED AND UP-AND-COMING AUTHORS TO THE ROUNDTABLE TO DISCUSS PERTINENT SOCIAL ISSUES, WRITING STYLES AND STEPS AUTHORS AND PUBLISHERS CAN TAKE TO CONNECT WITH BOOK CLUB MEMBERS MORE DEEPLY. HER COMMITMENT TO LITERARY EXCELLENCE AND BOOK CLUB STRENGTH IS UNCOMMON. I APPRECIATE JOY FARRINGTON AND ALL THAT SHE DOES TO SUPPORT BOOKS, LITERACY, COMMUNITY, AUTHORS AND WRITING!"

DENISE TURNEY

Just Write That Book Already!
AUTHOR OF *LONG WALK UP* AND HOST OF *OFF THE SHELF*

"I WAS SO BLESSED TO CONNECT WITH PROFESSIONAL AGENCIES SUCH AS YOURS WHICH HELPED ME TAKE MY LITERARY CAREER TO THE NEXT LEVEL. I AM SO LOOKING FORWARD TO WORKING WITH YOU IN THE FUTURE, AS I CAN'T IMAGINE MY MARKETING AND PROMOTIONAL EFFORTS NOT INVOLVING WORKING WITH YOU...ESPECIALLY IF I WANT THEM TO BE SUCCESSFUL."
—JOYLYNN JOSSEL, AKA E.N. JOY
AUTHOR OF THE *NEW DAY DIVAS* SERIES

"I HAD THE OPPORTUNITY TO WORK WITH JOY AT A BOOKSIGNING AND HAVE HER PROMOTE MY BOOK, *SECRETS UNRAVELED*. WHAT I LIKE ABOUT JOY IS THAT SHE IS A PROFESSIONAL AND CARES ABOUT YOU AS A PERSON AND WRITER. SHE HAS GREAT LEADERSHIP SKILLS AND KNOWS THE PUBLISHING INDUSTRY. I WOULD DEFINITELY WORK WITH HER ON FUTURE PROJECTS."
J.J. MICHAEL
AUTHOR OF *SECRETS UNRAVELED*

"I HAVE BEEN WORKING WITH JOY FARRINGTON OF LIT DIVA, INC. FOR A FEW MONTHS AND SHE IS A PLEASURE TO WORK WITH. HER PROFESSIONALISM AND KNOWLEDGE OF THE LITERARY WORLD IS EXCEPTIONAL. THE MARKETING STRATEGIES AND PACKAGES SHE OFFERS ARE PROFESSIONAL AND INEXPENSIVE. SHE IS SUPPORTIVE, A PLEASURE TO TALK TO AND I PRAY CONTINUED SUCCESS FOR HER AND LIT DIVA, INC."
LINDA Y. WATSON, AUTHOR OF *NECESSARY MEASURES*

Contents

Just Write That Book Already!

Once you initially work on each topic in your outline and have a few words on paper, the task of writing a book begins to seem less daunting and more manageable. Now is the time to back up, focus on each topic individually, and include details, history, and the information you researched for your book.

In general, your goal will be to write at least 25,000 to 50,000 words. This could generate an average 130 to 270 pages, depending on the book trim size. Book trim size is an industry term to describe the width and length of the book. The most standard book trims for non-fiction books are 6x9, 5x8, and 8x10.

To achieve your goal: Create a timeline...

Continues on page 41

This book was written for nonfiction writers and creative entrepreneurs. Fiction writers can successfully follow the practices found in this book. However, it does not address the many nuances of novel writing such as character development, plot, story exposition and other key ingredients to writing remarkable fiction.

ABOUT THE AUTHOR

Joy Farrington is the president of Lit Diva, Inc., a company that specializes in assisting coaches, speakers, and non-fiction authors with the writing, publishing, and marketing of their books. Her clientele includes bestselling authors and nationally renowned speakers. Her clients have been featured on Oprah, CNN, CNBC, FOX, BET, and the Huffington Post.

Joy is also an Amazon best-selling author and has written several books, including the co-authored *How to Write Your Book in 30 Days*, as well as the *e-Publishing Made Easy* series and the *Literary Diva Book Clubs* series.

Joy Farrington has been nominated for various awards, including the 3rd and 4th Annual Marguerite Press Awards for Best Promoter, Best Website, and Best Reviewer/Interviewer. She was also featured in the April 2005 issue of "Urban American Newspaper" as one of the 'Women in South Florida who … making moves in the Urban Community!!!'

Ms. Farrington has made it her goal to showcase the many facets of literature and book clubs through literary events, social networking and by encouraging readers to become more involved in the book community. She was the host of "In the

Spotlight," a literary teleseries that feature top-name authors. Her most famous interview to date was with acclaimed author, poet, and activist, Nikki Giovanni.

Ms. Farrington is also the co-facilitator of "Write Your Book in 30 Days" which was founded by Andrew Morrison, President of Small Business Camp. "Write Your Book in 30 Days" is a mastermind program created to assist entrepreneurs in creating a viable product in a month's time.

Introduction

Congratulations, you've made the decision to write a book, and you can't wait to get started! You bought a fancy new journal to jot down your notes, spent a whole day cleaning off your desk, and even added new songs to your playlist to get you in the writing mood. Now, it's the moment of truth.

You place your latte on the desk, turn on your laptop, open your new journal, and stare at the blinking cursor flashing on your computer screen. After a while, you begin to think the cursor is cursing at you in Morse code, and you become so intimated by its taunts you start losing your focus. Next thing you know, you log into Facebook "just to unwind for a sec," and your motivation to write has gone out the window.

Welcome to the world of writing.

In this age of fancy technology toys and social media overload, we face a sea of distractions:

TV, Music, Movies, Facebook Live, Podcasts, Games, iPhones, Text Messages, Skype, Email Alerts, Facebook, Twitter, Periscope, Candy Crush, Angry Birds, and the list goes on and on.

You also have your daily life and family obligations to contend with:

Your career, your kids' afterschool activities, trips to the gym, grocery shopping, doctor appointments, and weekly visits to your Great-Aunt Sally.

So between your smartphone beeping at you every five minutes with a new notification, your children asking for your help and needing it at that very moment, and your daily activities, when do you find the time to write?

Well, the short answer is: **you make the time.**

Many authors face the same obstacles; however, by making writing a priority, they're able to find the time to write regularly. The key is to put writing at the top of your to-do list.

As a Book Coach and Professional Book Accountability Partner, I work with authors, speakers, and coaches who all have a busy schedule. While working with my clients, I've discovered a majority of them get so fearful of the idea of writing a book, they avoid writing it as much as possible. Instead, they let their career, family life, and social distractions become their excuse as to why they never get any work done. If this sounds like you, this book is for you.

Since I want you to work on your book sooner rather than later, you won't find endless pages of filler information. Instead, this book was created in a workbook style format to help you get started on writing your book today.

Just Write That Book Already!

Writing a Book is the Easy Part

Writing a book is not difficult.

Stop laughing; I'm serious.

Writing a book isn't difficult because the help you need to write a book is readily obtainable. What many potential authors aren't aware of is the many tricks, tips, information, and support available to you. They're books such as this one that offer you information about the writing process. You can also enlist the help of a book coach, writing critique group, listen to audio courses, enroll in a writing course, or use my all-time favorite tool, Google, to search the Internet for writing tips. The support and information you need to learn how to write a book are available to you in many forms.

No, writing a book is not difficult; it's getting started that's a killer.

According to a 2002 survey conducted by the Jenkins Report, 81% of Americans feel there's a book inside of them. They want to write a book but how many actually do? For example, they might make a New Year's resolution to complete their book by March 1st. But by January 15th, because the idea of writing a book seems so overwhelming, they never put words to paper.

Have you ever sat in front of the computer to write but received so many distractions: Facebook, Twitter, text messages, your phone ringing off the hook and your children knocking on your bedroom door, you're fortunate if you write a paragraph? Distractions alone could be a killer in reaching your writing goal. However, at the end of the day, don't let those distractions stop you from writing.

As a Book Coach, I hear all kinds of excuses why a person didn't reach their weekly writing goal. But, it all boiled down to this: that person was either not mentally prepared, unorganized, or just so scared of failure they never made the extra push needed to work on their book.

Many people face this; you'll be surprised. Even authors who have several books under their belts suffer from fear of failure. Sometimes the idea of writing Chapter 1 can leave you with such an overwhelming feeling that you never make it to Chapter 2. It could be because you subconsciously know once you complete your book, then it's time for someone to actually (gasp) read it.

To become a successful author, you have to write, write, and then write some more. When you're not writing, you should be thinking about what you're going to write next. Once you get into the habit of writing, it should become second nature to you.

Writing is a craft, which means you have to hone your skills regularly. Again, join a writers' group or attend a few writing classes. Subscribe to Writers Digests. Read books by your favorite authors and dissect the elements of their books to better understand the components that make for a successful book in your genre.

Your job from now on is to appreciate that writing is an art form. Once you recognize the passion and dedication that created your favorite book, you'll have a better understanding of what it takes to be an author.

Your Family and Friends are holding you back

Yes, I know that's a harsh statement, but for many people, it's true. Your family and friends may be the reason you can't get one sentence written on a page. They don't mean to, and they don't even know they're doing it. However, let's face it; your children have an inept ability to know just when to interrupt you.

You know what I'm talking about. The moment when your muse finally decided to show up and your fingers are typing at the speed of light. Just when you're about to write the one sentence that will not only change the face of the literary world forever but also make you a million dollars to boot, your 12-year-old chose that moment to ask if you can take them to their BFF's (best friend forever) house. You give your daughter a noncommittal gruff and quickly get back to work when your cell phone begins to ring.

The shrill of the phone becomes such a distraction; you're forced to look at the caller ID and, seeing it's your brother, you answer the phone thinking something must be wrong. Something has to be wrong because you told him that very morning you plan to work on your book all day that day. Therefore, you rush to answer the call only to find out he just wanted to know whether you knew what happened to his high school yearbook. At this point, your muse has left the building and being the temperamental goddess that she is, refuses to come back until you get your act together. Now you're staring at that stupid blinking cursor, and no matter how hard you try, you just can't pick up where you left off.

The moment when your muse is standing behind you sending you positive, creative energy and encouraging you to write is what many people call the Writing Zone. It's a moment in time when you write without thinking; when all the planets align, and you know exactly what to write without hesitation. However, when you've been pulled abruptly out of the Writing Zone, it's the very dickens to get back.

So, you may become cranky at your daughter or slam the phone down in an indignant manner straight from a 1930s movie; but you can't be blamed for your behavior because you were just pulled out of the zone and how dare they do that to you. You are a writer, an artiste; handle with care.

Many creative entrepreneurs face the same problem you do. Your family and friends just don't get you. They don't understand how much the term "do not disturb" means to a creative. How the slightest distraction can throw you off your groove, and it can be difficult getting it back.

If indeed you are facing this problem, it's time to make a public declaration. Let everyone know you are writing a book and how your goal will affect your schedule from this day forward. Next, make it clear this isn't a hobby you just decided to pick up. Writing a book is not something you decided to do after watching a late-night infomercial. You have to treat writing like a second job, and your loved ones need to respect it as such.

It's going to be a difficult transition. Your children see mommy and daddy are home, so they assume their parents are readily available to them. They don't know you're lost in the world you created in your mind.

So talk to them and let them know this is a team effort. You need to get your family on your team because you need their support. When you hit a rough patch, and you turn into your Grumpy Gus persona, or when they see you walking around the house, with your head down mumbling to yourself about imaginary people, your family won't wonder if they should get you a straitjacket.

Talk to kids before starting your book and let them know you may be shutting them out mentally from time to time but it's only because you're in the Writing Zone and you haven't abandoned them. Set clear boundaries and explain to them the difference between issues that needs to be dealt with now vs. something you can handle later. For example, interrupting you because they can't find the TV remote doesn't qualify as an emergency.

Also, let your family know that since over the next few months you're going to be writing a book, they're going to have to make some sacrifices during this time. That includes asking your spouse to help with some chores or telling your sister you can't babysit your nephew every Saturday evening.

It means you're going to have to bail out on cocktail hours with the girls or tailgating with the boys. Your family and friends may not take your sudden change in behavior lightly. Yes, some will support you immediately; for others, it may take a while before they jump on board.

However, you will have those who won't support you at all. The Haters. They are going to be the ones who call you daily during your writing time and only during your writing time. They'll be the ones who always refer to your book as "that thing you're working on" almost as if they don't really believe you're actually working on anything. They're going to be mad at you because you can't go to the club every Friday night like you used to, going to the movies is the thing of the past, and going out for drinks…fuggedaboutit! You're a lean, mean writing machine and some of your friends just won't get the new you.

If this is indeed the case, prepare yourself because you may have to make a hard choice. You might have to decide what's more important: your friendship or your dream. In my opinion, if you have a friend who doesn't support you and actually goes out of their way to demean your dreams and passion, it's an easy decision.

Hopefully one day they do get how important your book is to you but for those friends that won't support your dreams and act in ways that almost sabotage your writing schedule, well, maybe it's time to clean up shop and get a new set of friends.

Myths Debunked

If you're feeling nervous about writing your book, give yourself permission to take it step by step. All you need to do is work at a steady pace, one word, one sentence, and one paragraph at a time. Eventually, you will complete your book before you know it.

However, if you don't think you have the skills it takes to write a book, I'm here to debunk a couple of myths for you.

Myth #1: It takes special talent to write a book

Wrong. It takes persistence to write a book. Yes, you have legends such as Tolkien, Butler, Angelou, and Hemmingway, who put the 'W' in Writer. However, writers write in various ways, shapes, forms, and you don't need any special talent to write a book. Nor do you need to be highly educated with a journalism degree or doctrine.

Many successful authors have never attended college, and some have never graduated from high school. If you can write in a clear and concise way, you can write a book. So no, you don't need a special talent to write a book. What you do need is a passion for your book topic, the desire to learn how to create a book, and dedication to complete the project.

Myth #2 Authors eventually starve in Garrets

Some authors only sell books to their family and friends. Others earn an additional stream of income by publishing 1-2 books a year. Then you have those who make the kind of money which we all dream of.

If you decide to make a career of writing nonfiction books, if choose your book's topic with care, your book can stay relevant for many years.

If you published with a publisher, for each year your book is in print, you get two royalty checks. Let's say you write two books a year for five years. At the end of the five years, if your books all stay in print, you'll be getting ten royalty checks a year. These continuing royalties are your nest egg, profitable investments in your future.

But, if you decide to self-publish your book (which I recommend all my clients to do), the profit you make is only limited by your commitment to promoting your book. In particular, if you're a speaker, coach, or trainer and you conduct workshops and seminars, you can earn secondary income by selling your books at the end of the event (these products are better known as back-of-the-room sales). As a self-published author, you cut out the middleman, the publisher, and retain all the net profits.

Regardless of how you publish your book or how many books you write, the sum of money you make will mainly be based on your efforts. And since I don't know anyone who lives or even owns a garret, chances are you don't have to worry about starving in one.

What Should I Write About?

The first step when writing your book is to get your book idea (book theme) clearly defined. If you already have an idea for your book, that's wonderful. However, what if you can't quite figure out what your book will be about?

There's nothing mysterious about devising ideas. Your ideas start with YOU. When you think about what you enjoy, about your experiences and your knowledge, you're guaranteed a regular fountain of ideas. It's only a matter of turning that fountain on.

Searching for ideas alerts your subconscious mind that ideas are important to you. Over the next few days, you may get a nudge from an idea, which says, "Write me down." Listen to your subconscious and write your idea down right away. Even if you're in the middle of a shower or you're driving down the highway (if you are driving, pull over or better yet, use the recording on your smartphone to record your thoughts).

The moment you have an idea, immediately record or jot it down despite how random or crazy that idea may be. Even if you're 100% sure you'll never in this lifetime forget that excellent idea you just had; believe me, you will. So, get in the habit of writing down your ideas.

Include personal testimonials and stories to highlight how you and others have overcome similar problems like the ones your readers are facing. By sharing your story, you make your book more personal, and you place yourself in the position of "learn from my mistakes and success." Many people like to learn from experts who experience the same pitfalls as them. So if you had a setback, share that as well. It will only drive down the overall message in your book even more.

Use the Idea Generators worksheets on the following pages to help you formulate your ideas. You can

Just Write That Book Already!

*complete all the worksheets provided
or only the one that you feel best fits
your book.*

Make a list of everything you excel in. Maybe you're good at buying presents for others, or you have a knack for choosing just the right shade of paint for your home. Maybe you're a fantastic home cook, an excellent swimmer, or a great tennis player. Or, is there something you used to be good at in the past? For example, were you a great gardener. But, because you no longer have a backyard you haven't gardened in years. If you have a green thumb, add it to the list.

_____

_____

_____

_____

_____

_____

YOUR EXPERIENCES

Experiences sell. People have written books about their business success and setbacks, their addictions, and even their pets. Use the following worksheet to jot down the significant experiences you had in the past. Work through this exercise quickly by setting a timer for 10 minutes and limit each experience to no more than a few sentences each.

_____

_____

_____

_____

_____

_____

_____

Read the newspaper and take note of trends. Better yet, listen to what your children are talking about and pay attention to what they're asking you to buy for them. By some weird, yet amazing internal beacon, children tend to like the same things at the same time before adults are even aware "that thing" exist. However, beware; the current hot topics may be old news before your book is in the stores. This doesn't mean you can't write on perennial favorites like money, sex, and exercise. These topics never go out of style, and a new twist on a popular topic is almost always a sure bet. However, if you're going to focus on writing about a current event, try to stay on top of the trend and catch the wave before it reaches its peak.

_____

_____

_____

_____

_____

You face challenges daily. Most are minor, yet some are unfortunately major obstacles. However, whatever your challenge is, whether it's moving to a new country or confronting a life threatening illness, others face the same problems and in that challenge lay the seeds of a book.

Use this worksheet to write some challenges you've encountered in your life from losing your job and facing bankruptcy to the betrayal of a spouse. After you complete the list, begin thinking about what obstacles you faced that can be a teachable moment or inspiration to others.

_____

_____

_____

_____

_____

_____

Your Passion

What do you love? What is your passion? People have written about garage sales, cosmetics, cars, vacations. Personally, I'm a self-proclaimed book addict. I love to read and enjoy sharing my love for books with others. That's why I wrote my first book, titled *A Literary Diva's Guide to Hosting a Fab Book Club Meeting*, which became an Amazon Best-Seller. Writing the book gave me an excuse to write about my passion for reading.

So, what are you passionate about?

_____

_____

_____

_____

_____

_____

_____

YOUR EXPERTISE

What is your expertise? Does your friend treat you like a Game Show Trivia lifeline and call to ask you random questions about pop culture? Do you sell more houses than any other realtor in the Tristate area? Can you organize a closet like nobody's business? Can you rebuild an engine with your eyes close? List the subject(s) that you're an expert in and use your background and experience as the basis for your book.

_____

_____

_____

_____

_____

_____

CHECKLIST: IS IT THE RIGHT BOOK IDEA FOR YOU?

After you worked through one or all the exercises, narrow your ideas to one primary theme. This idea will be used as your book topic.

Use the checklist below to determine whether the central idea you chose will work for you and your book:

- o Am I enthusiastic enough about this subject and my ideas to sell my books to my readers?
- o Does my book provide solutions to my reader's problems?
- o Will I retain my enthusiasm for the months it will take me to complete the book?
- o Is there a market for my book? Have I checked Amazon and bookstores for competing book titles, and I'm convinced there is a market for my book?
- o Can I find people with expert knowledge to interview as I write my book?

If you answered yes to all of these questions, you found the topic for your book.

Once you selected your book topic, the next step is to focus on a niche. A niche is a focus segment in a particular market. For instance, if you love gardening, you might write about how to start a garden in an urban neighborhood. Gardening is the idea or theme of your book and starting a garden in an urban area would be the niche.

To find a niche, pick a book topic with a problem attached to it.

For example, writing about ways busy moms can learn how to fit a healthy lifestyle into their schedule would be a niche with a problem attached to it. Going back to the gardening example; starting a garden in an urban neighborhood could be a problem because of the limited ground space typically available in a large city. Especially, in comparison to a rural neighborhood.

Once you pick a niche, identify the group of people who will have an emotional commitment to pay you money to solve their problem. This is your target audience, and these are the readers who will buy your book.

The Write

Technique

The **WRITE** Technique is the primary writing tool I teach my coaching clients. You can implement it to help you get started in organizing your book topics so you can begin writing, right away.

The **WRITE** Technique

Write an outline based on your theme
Research the topic, audience, and market for your book
Identify your audience and their problem
Teach your readers the solutions to their problem
Engage them with your story

Once you have chosen your book topic (Idea Generator Worksheets), create a working title for your book. It doesn't have to be perfect, and you'll probably change it several times throughout the book writing process. Don't worry about creating the perfect title. Instead, devise a title you can use to quickly reference your book.

Next, create an outline for your book by breaking the subject of your book into individual topics.

The main subject of your book should be the problem your reader is facing.

Therefore, each bullet point in your outline should be a solution to that problem.

Your outline will then become the chapters of your book and will help you during the writing process.

Expand on each topic in your outline using the knowledge you already have about the topic.

Write as much about each bullet point in your outline as possible without checking the Internet, referencing books or conducting interviews. At this stage in the game, the goal is to get all the information you already have about the topic on paper.

Once you've completed your first draft, review your manuscript (a term used to describe a book before it is published), and make a note of where you can add data and more information. Next, integrate the researched material into your book.

Writing a chapter of a book is like writing a long article. Most chapters are between 2000 and 4000 words, but if you want to write shorter chapters, that's fine too. Remember, it's your book, and you are making your own writing choices.

Don't focus too much on the formatting or correct grammar while writing your first draft. In the beginning, your initial goal is just to write.

Worry about the schematics later.

Once you initially work on each topic in your outline and have a few words on paper, the task of writing a book begins to seem less daunting and more manageable.

Now is the time to back up, focus on each topic individually, and include details, history, and the information you researched for your book.

In general, your goal will be to write at least 25,000 to 50,000 words. This could generate an average 130 to 270 pages, depending on the book trim size. Book trim size is an industry term to describe the width and length of the book. The most standard book trims for non-fiction books are 6x9, 5x8, and 8x10.

To achieve your goal:

> ➢ Create a timeline based on the number of words you plan to write each day; or
> ➢ Set aside a minimum of 60 minutes a day, two 30-minute time blocks; or
> ➢ Go hardcore and write for 2 to 8 hours a day, until you reach your goal.

After you complete your book, read and self-edit, then read and self-edit, then read and self-edit again until you're at the point when you're ready to throw your laptop out the window.

Once you have created the cleanest version of your manuscript possible, now it's time to hire a book editor (if you plan to self-publish) or find a book agent.

Find your Writing Technique

The same way everyone learns differently is the same way everyone writes differently. How Johnny goes about writing his book may be different from how Jane writes hers.

For example, this book is a product of three distinct styles.

Most of this book was outline prior to me writing each chapter. While writing this book, I added chapters not previously outlined while freestyling or intuitively writing each section.

I even had a recording from a teleconference transcribed. I then integrated portions of that transcription into this book.

Neither format is wrong, and the final product you're now holding in your hands is proof of that.

In this section, I've outlined several writing techniques that may fit your style. Once you find the technique(s) that best fits you, follow the steps outlined to help you begin the writing process.

The *Write Your Book Technique* is an easy way to get started in organizing your book topics so you can begin writing right away.

Getting Started

First, create an outline for your book by breaking down the subject of your book into individual topics. As I mentioned before, the main subject of your book is the problem your reader is facing. So, each bullet point in your outline should be a solution to that problem. Your outline will then become the chapters in your book and will help you during the writing process.

Again, don't focus too much on the formatting or your grammar skills at first. In the beginning, your initial goal is to just write.

Expand on each topic in your outline using the knowledge you already have about the topic.

Once you initially work on each topic in your outline and have a few words on paper, the task of writing a book begins to seem less daunting and more manageable.

Now is the time to back up, focus on each topic individually, and include details, history, and the information you research for your book.

Use the Outline Worksheet located in the Book Map chapter to help you create an outline for your book.

Another way to write your book is by not writing it at all. If you feel more comfortable talking than writing, this process is ideal for you. Matter of fact, I know many speakers and coaches who use their "gift of the gab" to write their book in this matter. Even if you don't decide to record your entire book, this is a useful tool to use when you are on the go and don't have a pen, paper, or laptop with you.

Getting Started

As mentioned in Technique #1, write an outline for your book. Each chapter will be based on a topic you will record in details once your outline is completed.

1. Take a voice recorder (save money by using your voice recorder already built into your smartphone) and record yourself speaking about each topic.
2. Save the recording and send it to a transcriber.
3. Once the chapters have been transcribed, you can either (a) go

through each chapter and "fluff-up" the material or (b) hire a ghostwriter to do the task for you.

"Fluff-up" is a term I use to describe reworking your words so they contain more value, is coherent, and more reader-friendly.

You can also use previous recordings from past teleconferences, speeches, and so on, which can be used as a material for your book.

Technique #3: Storyboard Your Book

I like this process because it is relatively easy to follow and is ideal for those who like to stay organized and keep everything in its place. The *Storyboard Your Book Technique* will also help you better formulate ideas and keep track of your research.

Getting Started

1. Buy at least 2 to 6 packs of large index cards.
2. During a brainstorming session, write all your thoughts and ideas for your book on the cards. One idea or topic per card.
3. Once completed, separate the cards into categories of your choosing (e.g. by chapters).
4. Once separated into categories, put them in order of relativity.
5. Sort through each category and discard any idea that does not fit into your book.

You now have an outline for your book.

Again, create a timeline to write your book, and write every day using the information you wrote on the index cards.

Keep the index cards in an index card binder, box, or inside an index card ring (available in office supply stores). Then use the card to help you while writing each chapter.

As you come up with more ideas or resources you want to include in your book, write them on an index card for easy references.

You can also buy a large corkscrew board to help keep your note cards in order. Categorize your note cards and switch, move, or remove them from the board during your writing process.

Have you ever written an article? Do you have a blog? Did you keep the notes from a speaking engagement you held last year? If so, this is your intellectual property (any content that you've created and own the rights to). By looking at your old files, you will be surprised at the information you have created over the years. Therefore, do not overlook the work you have done in the past, as it can become a valuable tool you can use in your writing and beyond.

Getting Started
1. Take stock of your inventory (previous works).
2. Gather all the information into a binder, index card ring. You can also create a file folder on your computer.
3. Organize each intellectual property by subject.
4. Once completed, go through the files to see what could be integrated into your book. For example, you can take the recording from a previous teleconference or interview you have conducted and have it transcribed. Now you have a new chapter for your book—not too complicated, huh?

5. Expand on each item you add to the book with new information and thoughts to help streamline the new addition to your chapter and help keep the same tone throughout the book.

Some examples of your intellectual property include:

➢ Speaking Notes
➢ Blog Postings
➢ Teleconference Recordings
➢ Interviews
➢ Transcripts
➢ Articles
➢ Podcast Shows
➢ Webinar Recording

A ghostwriter is someone you hire to either help you write portions of your book or write the entire book for you.

A ghostwriter's primary goal is to translate your ideas, thoughts, stories, and experience and turn it into a book.

Some will take the interviews they've conducted with you, and turn those sessions into a tangible book format. Others will use your notes and finesse them, so your ideas are more book ready.

Then you have ghostwriters that will do all the work for you from research to the end product.

Ghostwriters prices range based on the exact amount of work needed, combined with their years of experience. You could agree to pay the ghostwriter on the page, word count, time spent, or offer a percentage of the royalty. In doing research for this book, I came across prices ranging from $6,000 to $125,000.

Many celebrities, politicians, and well-known fiction authors use ghostwriters. Ever purchased a book with the term "as told by," "contributions by," or "with" on the cover? That's a good indication that a ghostwriter was involved in writing the book.

If and how a ghostwriter is credited will be part of the negotiation process. It could be a sentence written on the acknowledgment page. Their name listed underneath the author on the cover. Or, they receive no credit at all. A ghostwriter is just that—an invisible part of the book process. So, if and how you decide to credit the ghostwriter will be up to you and should be negotiated during the hiring process.

Some Tips for Hiring Ghostwriters:
Discuss the style and tone you want to convey in the book beforehand.

- Make sure it's clear who will own the rights to the book. And in case you have any doubts, that person is you. Make sure that's clearly stated in the contract

- Decide whether the ghostwriter will be credited in the book and if so, how they will be listed

- Ask to see their portfolio so you can get an idea of the type of writer they are (voice, tone, format, etc...) Don't be shy. Ask for references

- Create a fee schedule and agree to pay the writer in intervals of completion (25%, 50%, 75%, 100%). Definitely pay a deposit but don't pay the full amount till the work is completed

- If working with a firm, check the Writers Beware website to make sure the company is on the up and up. Consider finding ghostwriters on sites like www.Odesk.com. Again, check their portfolio and ask for references.

I don't care if you decide to hire your trusting Aunt Jenny, who attends church every Wednesdays and Sundays, to ghostwrite your book; don't proceed without a contract.

If and when your book becomes a success, and you have Hollywood knocking on your door, without a contract, Aunt Jenny could claim the rights to your book.

So once all the logistics are worked out, have the contract and a Confidently, and Disclosure agreement looked over by a lawyer before you begin working with a ghostwriter.

Book Map

Now is the time to create an outline, or what I like to call Book Map, of your book. You don't need to create the kind of outline that your English teacher harassed you to write when you were fifteen. The type of framework you need to create is one based on components.

Some consider non-fiction books easier to write than fiction because non-fiction books have easy-to-follow elements. Let's look at some of them:

Foreword

This is similar to an introduction, but a foreword is usually by someone other than the author of the book. It helps if you can get someone famous to contribute the foreword. Also, if you're writing in an area in which you don't have professional expertise—for example, if you're writing about a medical topic and you're not a doctor—then getting a foreword by a professional would be ideal.

Note: There's a very small possibility they may ask for payment for writing a foreword. If you think it's worth it, if this person could lend significant credibility to your book and your budget allows it, consider paying them for the foreword.

About the Book

This can be short or quite long. For example, if you're writing a book on yoga, you could use this chapter to give four or five exercise routines compiled from the various poses that you discuss in the rest of the book.

Introduction

This section is recommended but optional. Include an introduction if you want to tell your own story: how you came to get the information you're about to share or background information about the topic of the book.

Chapters

Outline the readers' problem in each chapter and offer a solution. For example, if you were writing a book on dieting, you could write seven chapters all posing a typical problem, then provide solutions to each problem.

Chapter 1: Keys to Weight Loss

Chapter 2: Why other Diet Programs Fail

Chapter 3: The Weight Loss System that will Change Your Life

Chapter 4: An Exercise Program for those who hate to Sweat

Chapter 5: If All Else Fails…

Chapter 6: What Your Grandmother should have told you about Dieting

Chapter 7: How to Stay on Track even when you Fall the Path

Conclusion

The last chapter is the wrap-up. In this chapter, you'll want to give readers instructions on where they go from here, and you'll also want to include an inspirational message.

Glossary

A glossary is useful if it will be necessary for readers new to the subject area. For example, if your book contains plenty of industry jargon with which your reader is unfamiliar, explain the terminology here.

Index

If you think your readers would find it useful, go the extra mile and include an index. Also, if you plan to sell your books to libraries, an index is a huge selling point.

Chapter by Chapter

Let's now dig deeper into each chapter structure and walk through the structure for a typical book beginning with the title. Your reader has a problem, and your book title offers a benefit. Here's a stat I want you to consider: nearly 70% of all books that are purchased are never even read. Yes, you read correctly, 70% of all books that are purchased are never read past maybe 5 or 10 pages. So, why did that person buy the book?

They bought the book because the title spoke to their particular problem at the time. So your book cover, your title has to speak to that particular problem. That's one of the deciding factors in why a person buys a book. They buy books because of the cover and because of the title. There should be no shame in that game. I want you to understand the game and make sure your title is compelling and speaks to solving a particular problem.

Inside the book, you have your chapter title but consider adding a quote to the beginning of each chapter. There's a ton of online resources that will give great quotes that relate to the chapter title. In the appendix, I've included a list of websites that you can use to help you find a suitable quote for your book.

Next, let's look at how you should structure the chapters in your book.

Create the heading for your chapter. Your heading for your chapter could be a solution to solving a problem. Once you have a heading for your chapter, begin writing about the concept for that heading. At first, just write what you know. You can also go back and add facts and details later but for now, get in the habit of pouring out all your knowledge onto paper first, then going back and fine-tuning that information.

Afterward, read through your chapter and see if you address the concept behind the solution or behind this chapter. If not, add more text to the chapter to make the concept clear to your readers. Next, make sure you defined industrial terms for your readers because you may have used jargon your reader is unfamiliar with. For example, you can't assume everybody knows what "PR" is.

Take the time to explain that PR is an abbreviation for Public Relations, and define what Public Relations means.

Once you define the term, you can begin using the jargon, or abbreviation, throughout the rest of the book. But as mentioned before, don't fill your book with unnecessary jargon.

If you find yourself defining every other term in your chapter, it might affect the book readability. And never feel afraid that you're writing too basic. Your readers will each come to you at different learning levels, starting with beginners. There are always readers who need some basic information, and your definitions are critical.

So, you just define your chapter heading. If you haven't done so already, begin adding facts into the chapter. You always want to have some facts to prove you really are an expert on the book's topic.

There's a great website called fedstats.gov where you can find industry statistics you can include in your book.

After you integrate data to your book, write a story. People love stories. Stories sell. So, tell a story that affirms the concept behind your chapter. Your story could be a testimonial from a client, a summary of an event that happened in your life or maybe even an article from an expert in your field. In the end, you could mention the moral of the story. Then, explain how they could apply the moral of the story, into their everyday life.

Finally, close with an exercise or plan of action.

Let's suppose your book is titled *20 Things You Need to Know Before you Buy your First Home*, and chapter 3 is titled "Know your Neighborhood."

You could include a quote that's interesting, motivational, or funny. Then, you'd define the concept behind your chapter heading. You told your reader they should "Know your Neighborhood." What do you mean by that? Are you saying they need to drive around the neighborhood, research the neighborhood statistics such as schools, crime rates, and get an overall feel about their neighbors before moving in? If that's what you're referring to, write it down. Break your chapter heading or concept to the lowest decibel for your reader so, by the end of the chapter, they know exactly what you mean when you say, "Know your Neighborhood."

After you break down your chapter concept, go back and define any terms you used. For instance, when you discussed the stats in a neighborhood, did you use the term "Per capita"?

Well, let your readers know what Per capita means, in case they're not familiar with the terminology.

Finally, add facts and statistics to back up why you encouraged your reader to become familiar with a neighborhood before they make the final decision to buy a home.

Either within or at the end of the chapter, you could reinforce your chapter topic by adding a testimonial or story from a previous client about how they either wish they looked into their neighborhood first before buying a home or why they're glad they took your advice and checked out the neighborhood before purchasing their house.

Let's dissect your book *even* further.

Title Page

Required: Your title page should include the title and subtitle of your book, your name and if you like, the name of the publishing company. You could also include an image that reflects your book title or replicates your book cover and use it as your title page.

Short Blurbs (Testimonials)

Optional: Here you can include some testimonial from your peers, readers, and clients. These testimonials or blurbs should be kept to a few sentences. Make sure to include the name of the person who wrote it, their credentials, their website.

Example:

"*Just Write That Book Already!* has changed the way I now write my books."
—Jack Canfield, bestseller author of the *Chicken Soup for the Soul Series*
www.chickensoup.com

Ok, ok, so I made that particular blurb up. But heck you never know, Jack Canfield may actually think my book is just that great.

Copyright Page
Required: The copyright page should include the year your book was copyrighted, and by whom (either you or your publisher). The page should look similar to this:

Copyright © XXXX by XXXXXXX

All rights reserved. No part of this book may be reproduced or transmitted in any form or by any means without written permission from the author.

ISBN 13: XXXXXXXXXX
ISBN 10: XXXXXXXXX

Limits of Liability and Disclaimer of Warranty
The author and publisher shall not be liable for your misuse of this material. This book is strictly for informational and educational purposes.

Warning – Disclaimer

The purpose of this book is to educate and entertain. The author and/or publisher do not guarantee that anyone following these techniques, suggestions, tips, ideas, or strategies will become successful. The author and/or publisher shall have neither liability nor responsibility to anyone with respect to any loss or damage caused, or alleged to be caused directly or indirectly by the information contained in this book.

Dedication

Optional: Usually written in 1-2 sentences, briefly write whom you'd like to dedicate your book to.

Acknowledgement

Optional: Consider this your Oscar winning speech. Here, you'll list everyone who helped you complete your book.

Preface

Optional: A preface is an optional section in your book and is usually written by someone other than the author, such as a celebrity or industry expert. It discusses the relationship between the person writing the preface, the author, the value of the book, and how the reader will benefit from reading it. You could compare this to having someone co-sign your bank loan. It helps your reader build trust in you when someone praises your knowledge.

Introduction

Highly Recommended: The introduction is your chance to talk about why you decided to write your book. This is also an opportunity for you to discuss who you are (your credentials, and background), what the book is about in details, and what you hope the reader will take away after reading your book.

Write your introduction in such a way that if someone was browsing through your book in the bookstore and glanced at these few pages, they will be compelled to buy your book.

Chapter 1

Required: Your reader picked up your book because they have a problem they have to solve and are hoping your book will address their needs.

In the first chapter, your goal is to discuss your reader's problem and assure them your book will address it head-on.

Discuss what they may be worried about, their uncertainties, and their fears. Then reassure them that you will be able to help with their problem. When writing this section, imagine yourself walking with your reader up a cliff. Although you both see the hard path laid ahead, you continue to encourage your walking partner by letting them know you took this journey before and you know that just beyond those trees, the path will suddenly even out, and it's smooth sailing ahead.

Chapter 2-3

Required: By Chapter 2 or 3, you should begin the process of discussing the plan you created to help them solve their problem. Use funny anecdotes, personal stories, and testimonies as a way to better connect with your readers.

Additional Chapters

Required: After you calm their fears and outline a plan, begin offering them a solid foundation they can continue to follow, long after they finish your book.

In these chapters, describe in more details 1) your plan, 2) resources they can rely on, and 3) tools they need to solve their problem. These chapters are the reason why your reader bought your book. Since you are offering the most valuable content in these chapters, make sure you write clearly and concisely.

Final Chapter(s)

Required: This is the chapter(s) where you offer them a contingency plan in case they're unable to follow through with the steps you provided for them.

For example, a diet book would offer encouraging words to help motivate the reader to keep going; even if they fall off the diet. Again, include a story or testimony to illustrate everyone is human and even you, the author, fall off track from time to time.

Conclusion

Required: Here, you'll wrap up your book by referencing key points you mapped out in your book, and actions they should take after they finish it.

Consider adding a couple of resources (especially your website). You could write the conclusion in a celebratory tone congratulating them for sticking it through to the end, or give them inspirational words to live by.

About the Author Page

Recommended: In this section, you will include your author bio and a call to action (website address, email address, phone number, etc.).

Product Pages

Recommended: Create product pages highlighting your products and services. List one product page per product or service. Include a call to action clearly written, preferably at the bottom of the page.

Index:

Recommended: The index is a quick reference guide located at the back of your book based the word or term listed in the book. If you plan to sell your book to the library, you should include an Index in your book.

*Create an outline for your book. To
help you get started, use the
worksheet on the following page.*

Title Page
Copyright Page
Dedication
Acknowledgment

Table of Content

Foreword

About This Book

Introduction

Chapter 1 Primary Topic:
Main Points (Support your main points
throughout each chapter):

(Support your main points throughout
each chapter)

Chapter 2 Primary Topic:
Main Points:

Chapter 3 Primary Topic:
Main Points:

Chapter 4 Primary Topic:
Main Points:

Chapter 5 Primary Topic:
Main Points:

Chapter 6 Primary Topic:
Main Points:

Chapter 7 Primary Topic:
Main Points:

Chapter 8 Primary Topic:
Main Points:

Chapter 9 Primary Topic:
Main Points:

Chapter 10 Primary Topic:
Main Points:

Chapter 11 Primary Topic:
Main Points:

Chapter 12 Primary Topic:
Main Points:

Conclusion

Bibliography
About the Author
Product Page
Glossary
Index

How to Write an

Interview Style Book

Interview-style books are surprisingly popular. They are also very easy to create. Interview style books are just what the namesakes suggest. They are books that are primarily written by interviewing an expert or experts and chronicling the interview into book format.

The easiest way to interview your expert is my using a free teleconference service to record the interview.

Once the interview is complete, save the recording (most services have an option for you to save and download the call as an audio file). Next, download the file. Then send it to your favorite transcriber. Once the transcription is complete, read through the document and pull out any excerpt you feel your readers will find interesting. Also, remove any non-essential words like "um."

Once you are satisfied with the content, send your manuscript to an editor. He or She will edit your book and make sure it doesn't read as one endless conversation without a concise beginning, middle, and end.

Writing an Interview Book is one of the shortest books you can produce and can even be ready for publication in a matter of days.

1.The Interview Stage

Know what your book's specific slant and topic is going to be *before you start interviewing people.* That way, your questions will be targeted to extract the most relevant and interesting information from for your readers.

This holds true even if you are planning to create your book from interviews already recorded or completed. Simply go through your past recordings and pull out:

- the information relevant to the main topic; and
- human interest stories that will make the reader identify and humanize your expert.

Funny anecdotes and interesting facts will ensure your reader to you and the expert(s) you interviewed.

2. Give Your Interview Candidates an Incentive to Participate

A few interview candidates will do it just for the publicity. But also offer to include a link to their own websites, offers or bonuses in your book.

3. Your Book Structure

Here are essential elements you need to include in your Interview-Style book:

- Add a professional photo of the expert you interviewed to the cover of your book.
- When writing the Preface, include why you choose to interview the expert(s) or celebrities in the book.
- Mention how you became acquainted with them. Your history with the expert.
- Include any funny stories you think the readers may enjoy. Example: why the celebrity just so happens to be your first celebrity crush.

4. Make Your Interview Candidates Connect

It is crucial that your readers connect with your interview candidates. It is also vital that they view your subject as an authority figure. Here's how to make sure this happens:

- Include a short bio of the expert. If you are interviewing more than one person in your book, add each bio before or after each chapter. You could also include all your bios together in a chapter preceding your interviews.

- Focus on celebrity status details that will connect with the reader. So make sure you mention the fact your candidate appeared on Dr. Oz or holds the record as the first person to Livestream in all 50 States.

- Include a photo of your interview candidate. People feel more comfortable if they put a face to the name. You could add a headshot at the beginning of the chapter.

- Make sure any promotional information you share is reader-centered. The temptation is to stress your interview candidate's achievements—but only share details that the readers: 1) can connect with emotionally, 2) will find helpful, and 3) want to know.

5. Your Conclusion

The interviews should all combine to either support your topic or give a strong serving of specific niche information.

6. Optional

You can also include the following sections:

- **Contributors**: This is your last chance to acknowledge and promote your interview candidates (or other people who contributed to your book, but were not interviewed).

- **Resources**: This always adds value to a book, if you can recommend further reading, software, apps, services or websites that will enhance what the reader gets out of the book.

How to Write a How-to Book

How-to books will always sell.

Why?

Because people are always looking for the fast and easy way to get something done.

Want to learn how to use Instagram? There's a book for that.

Want to learn how to BBQ chicken? There are several books on that.

Want to organize that junk drawer you've kept hidden from your family? There's a book for that too.

Yes, you can go online and google all your questions and get the answer within seconds. Yet, people still love the promise of a book that will magically and instantly simplify their lives. A book that will solve their problems. A book just like the one you're reading now; one that will become your patient tutor and walk you through the process.

When writing your How-to Book, make sure the structure for each chapter are logical and consistent. Decide in advance if you need:

- Photos
- Diagrams

Or if you're just using in-text instructions. Decide in advance on the fonts, font sizes, colors and weight for your elements. For example, are you going to use:

a) The alphabet in your point indicators?

Or.

1) Numerals?

Ask yourself the following questions:

- How big will your Sub-Heads be?
- Will you leave room for your readers to write notes?

Is what you're demonstrating too small to be accurately shown in the image you're using?

- Exactly who are you going to teach?
- What problem are you solving for them?
- How much information do they need to know to solve the problem?
- What level are your readers in solving the problem? Beginners, Intermediate, Advance?

Your Book Structure

Start out with a Foreword, Introduction or an Introductory paragraph or two.

Write an About the Book section. Explain what problem(s) your book will address for the reader. This section will let the reader know they picked the right book.

Also, discuss what your reader will accomplish and the take away after completing your book. Finish with any general instructions they need to know to get the full benefits of your book.

Start each chapter by telling the reader what they are going to learn in that chapter

If your book is in eBook format, remember that any graphics or diagrams you include need to be clearly visible on a phone reading app such as iBooks or a Kindle Reader. Make sure they are simple, uncluttered and large as possible. (Go for the ultimate close up!)

When writing your chapters:

Demonstrate no more than one unit per chapter. For instance, write about one way of hemming a pant leg in Chapter One and showcase another method in Chapter Two.

An exception to this rule is if you are writing a comparison; in which case, each method would be presented and demonstrated in exactly the same fashion.

Simplify everything down to its essentials.

If you find yourself going off on a tangent or starting a whole separate topic, stop and reassess what your book topic is about.

If a section of your book complicates the book topic for your readers by introducing a new topic, remove the sections that may read like a tangent and put it in another document. You may have the makings of another book or series of books. So save the ideas for another writing day.

Your Book Conclusion

When you have finished your main chapters, end your book by summarizing what they learned, and confirming how it will benefit them.

Don't assume your reader will sail through your books and follow your instructions to a "T." Instead, offer them a failsafe way for them to jump back into the program you outline. Also share quick tips to correct any mistakes they may make along the way. Remind them that at the end of the day, we're all human, and life happens.

In the Conclusion, be sure to congratulate them on completing the book. Also, let them know where they can buy other books written by you, any programs you may have available, and a way to learn more and connect with you.

Writing a Tip Book

Aww, one of my favorite go-to books for gleaning information quickly and easily, The Tip book. I'm sure you've seen them. They are usually the books in the store with titles such as "7 Ways to Organize your Desk" or "101 Ways to kidnap a Dalmatian Puppy" (see what I did there).

But all jokes aside, this is possibly the easiest type of book you can write. This is also one of the most straight-forward books for readers to digest because the information is presented in concise, bite-size pieces.

For example, if your book title is *27 Ways to Set up your Roku Player*, the first chapter could be "Step One: Plug the USB plug into your TV." In this chapter, write a short section on how to complete step one.

Your Book Title

Your book title must contain two components: the <u>number</u> of tips you are offering in the book and a <u>solution word</u> such as "Way," "Tips," "Reasons Why," or "Types."

Examples:

7 Ways to Write a Book

7 Tips for Writing a Book

7 Reasons Why You Should Write a Book

7 Types of Books You Can Write Today

When doing Research for your Book

Make sure to cite all your sources in the Appendix of your book

Rewrite the information you find in your own words. Do not copy tips verbatim. That's copyright infringement—a huge no-no in the writing world.

One way to source your cite in your book is by mentioning the source in your subheading such as, "Here's 5 tips from Mrs. Butler's book, *How to Grow a Garden.*"

Your Book Chapters

Initially, write down your tips on flashcards.
Weed out duplicates. Organize your tips in order of relevance by placing them in three categories: Essential Tips, Lesser-known tips, and Insider Tips.

Essential tips are tips everyone needs to know, and for many readers—may know already. But, your essential tip will reassure the latter category of readers that you know what you're talking about.

Lesser-known tips are potentially highly valuable. These are the sort of tips that can make the reader say: "Wow. It was worth buying the book just for that tip!"

"Insider" tips are tips the reader wouldn't have found through regular channels. To offer these tips, you either need to: be an expert on the topic, research the heck out of the topic, or interview an expert on the topic.

You can either organize your tips in category order or offer them as a mix-bag. Also write your tips in strong, short sentences.

While Writing

Don't ramble.

Don't use unnecessary "filler" phrases that distract from your point.

Keep it short, concise, and to the point.

Write your sentences in an authorize tone. For example, "Using Palmolive Soap is a simple way to clean your silver." is a concise sentence. While, "I've heard that if you use Palmolive, you may be able to clean some of your silver." rambles a bit and is not written in an authorize tone.

Include a short Introduction and Conclusion to your book. Also, add an About the Author page so readers can learn more about you and your services.

Book Size

Tip books range in size based on the number of tips presented. Typically, Tip Books are small with an average of 20-40 pages.

How to Format Your Manuscript

The interior book design for a non-fiction book is different from a fiction book. For example, a non-fiction book may include pictures, comics, quotes and inspirational stories from other writers. Those same elements would be out of place in a fiction book.

- Use the Tab button on your keyboard instead of the space bar to indicate a new paragraph
- Double space your document
- Create a new page for each chapter
- Keep all chapters in one document instead of creating a new doc for each chapter
- Use italics instead of underlining words you would like to emphasize. Underline words sparingly for optimal effect
- Write The Title of a New Chapter by Alternating Capital Letters
- Avoid WRITING EACH CHAPTER TITLE IN ALL CAPS, which not only is considered screaming at your reader but is also hard on the reader's eyes.

WHEN FORMATTING YOUR BOOK FOR SUBMISSION TO AN AGENT OR PUBLISHING COMPANY:

- The Book Industry preference is to write and save your manuscript in a .doc .docx file (Microsoft Word)
- Set Margins at 1" top and bottom, flush left, with a 1.25 margin left and right, 0.5" paragraph Index
- Set line spacing to double space
- Number pages consequently on top right corner of each page
- Use Times New Roman font with a 12-point size
- Print on a 20lb white bond paper, size 8 ½ x11
- Keep pages loose, not bound in any fashion

Picking a Book Title

Using keywords in your book title is a strategic move to help rank your book in search engines as well as online bookstores. As authors, we have a tendency to want a clever, cute, and snazzy title. But, you should also consider if your title will instantly gain the attention of your reader by addressing their problem. If not, it doesn't matter how unique your title is if it's not helping you sell your book.

KISS (Keep it Simple, Silly)

Keep your book title short and to the point. Dan Poynter, bestselling author of *Writing Nonfiction* and *The Self-Publishing Manual*, suggests you keep your title to 92 characters, about 5 to 6 words. My first book was titled *A Literary Diva's Guide to Hosting a Fab Book Club Meeting*. In hindsight my clever, cute, and snazzy, the title was too long (I'm sorry, Dan). It took up too much space on the book cover and was hard to shorten without losing the essence of the book.

Some Real Life Examples of great book titles:
1. *Become a Highly Successful Sought after VA*
2. *Guerrilla Marketing for Writers*
3. *The Zen of Social Media Marketing*
4. *The 4-day Work Week*

Be Specific

In today's marketing world, it all about having a niche and targeting your audience. Express your niche in the title such as the *Working Mom's Guide to Staying Sane or Living on a Budget for College Students.* Let your title speak to your audience and use it as a selling point for your book.

Let your Subtitle Do All the Hard Work

Your subtitle should be descriptive and encompass what the buyer will learn after reading your book.

Some real life examples:
1. A complete reference guide to starting a successful and PROFITABLE virtual assistant business
2. 100 No-Cost, Low-Cost Weapons for Selling Your Work

3. An Easier Way to Build Credibility, Generate Buzz, and Increase Revenue

Play on Words

Book titles can't be copyrighted, which is why you may (and will) find the same titles for different books. I don't recommend you use the exact title from another book because 9 times out of 10 you could end up losing books sales in the midst of all the confusion.

But I do suggest creating a play on words of a popular title to help increase the popularity and ranking of your book. This is a great marketing tool that you can use later on down the publishing road.

For example, comedian and bestselling author Steve Harvey's first book was entitled *Act like a Lady, Think like a Man.* Author Shanae Hall wrote a relationship book and named it *Why do I have to Think Like a Man? How to Think Like a Lady and Still get the Man.* Her play on words helped her sell more books online since Amazon automatically paired it with Steve Harvey's book.

TRICKS OF THE TRADE

Keep your title positive by focusing on the benefits of your book. Avoid words like "Don't" and "Not" in the title.

Test different titles to see which one garners the most interest. Send out a survey, testing several titles by using Survey Monkey or use social media sites like Twitter and Facebook and ask your social friends and fans to vote for their favorite.

Book titles can't be copyrighted, but trademarks are a different story. Don't use someone else's trademark in your title. For example, the *Chicken Soup for the Soul* book series is a branded trademark. If you have any doubts, visit http://www.uspto.gov/ and conduct a quick trademark search before settling on a title.

After visiting http://www.uspto.gov, conduct a thorough search on Google and Amazon to make sure no one is using the same book title.

Think about your book cover design when picking a title. When I think about *Working Mom's Guide to Staying Sane,* I see a frenzy looking woman sitting at her desk which is stacked with paperwork; with her high-on-sugar kids, impatient husband, and mean boss nearby. What image do you see when you think about your title?

Off the top of my head, I can't remember who wrote *Free,* or who was the creator of the *...for Dummies* book series. But I have read those books several times and know them from the inside out. Readers remember titles before they remember the author's name, so make your title memorable.

Action Plan: Create 3-5 titles of your book and post it in my Writer Mastery Community Facebook group. Ask members to vote on their favorite. Include keywords in your title. You can find keywords based on your target audience and industries by visiting Google Keyword tool at http://alturl.com/e39qf. It will list the amount of traffic it receives for each keyword you enter and even break the websites that use those keywords down by demographics.

Side Note: I created the titles *Working Mom's Guide to Staying Sane* for the purpose of this book. If you like them, feel free to use it. In exchange, please consider naming your first child after me. I'll also take cash; preferably in untraceable bills.

Research the Topic, Audience, and Market for your Book

Fiction authors and nonfiction authors research their topic differently, but despite which genre you're writing in, you do have to do some sort of research for your book.

Nonfiction authors are expected to do more industry and data research. Their research may include reading magazines, books, newspaper articles, industry blogs, reports, and even federal data. Whereas a fiction author researches information to supplement their storyline such as landmarks in the city their characters are located in, the procedure for arresting a suspect, or how to bake a lemon meringue pie. In essence, a nonfiction author gathers facts to reinforce the information they have written in their book while a fiction author gathers facts to make their characters, setting, and story more believable.

Where you get your information from and how you use it will depend greatly on the type of book you're writing. However, whether it's a textbook, workbook, novel, booklet, nonfiction, historical romance, biography or memoir, there are two types of sources you will be accessing: primary and secondary sources.

Primary data is information that comes straight from the source, whereas secondary data is information you found, which reference another source. Keep track of all the information you gathered by creating a Work Cited page. Once you finish writing your book, make sure you included a bibliography or Work Cited form in your book (for nonfiction books or fictions authors, creating a work cited page isn't necessary unless you specifically use the information you gather, such as quote from another book).

You can write the information you found by hand in a notebook, on individual index cards, or use a Word document to keep track of your information.

Also, while you're outlining your book, make a note of any topic(s) you need to research. You can do this my making a notation in a notebook while you're writing your first draft or after you read your manuscript for the first time. The outline is to give you a handy tool to use during the resource process.

If you're anything like me, a trip to the library or bookstore to do some research will turn into anything but research. By having a print out of your outline or mind map with you, it will be less tempting to explore other avenues. These avenues may well be informative, but for other projects, not the one you're currently working hard to compete.

Once you start writing, your only goal should be to "get it done." If you can't take a trip to the library (and to be quite honest, it's not as necessary as it used to be), **do a general search on the Web using a search engine like Google.com to locate areas you could explore**.

Strive to find the primary source of the information you use in your book. For example, an article from Wikipedia is secondary data but the sources the writer use for the article is (more than likely) the primary source. When writing a book, you're responsible for the information provided on those pages; it's your responsibility to make sure the data is correct by finding the original source.

While doing your research, if you find any online groups or mailing lists, which seem appropriate for your subject, join them. The members may be able to provide you with anecdotes or other information.

Make a note of companies which are mentioned in your Web search. Can they help you? The benefit of asking companies to assist you in your research is, they can provide you with free and the most current information. Most companies will be only too pleased to help, even if it's just for the PR boost you can give them. Make a note to yourself to acknowledge them in your book. If any company has given you plenty of help, it's nice gesture to send them a copy when the book is published.

Check periodical indexes for articles which might be useful. Once you needed to trudge along to the library for this kind of help, but LexisNexis (www.lexis.com) is faster.

Are there any books which could help you? Try www.amazon.com to find recent books on your topic. (You may already have notes on these books, which you collected while you were attempting to formulate an idea for a book.)

Conduct Interviews. Make a note of people you will want to interview for your book and reach out to them. Now's a good time to take a stroll through your contact list. You may be surprised who you currently have in your Rolodex.

When you're completed writing your book, add Bibliography (the Work Cited page) at the end of the book by clicking Reference tab and under the Citations & Bibliography section, click the Bibliography page.

The purpose of researching your market is to see what books are out there based on your book topic. It's also to find out how sellable your topic is and if readers will be interested in your book. So when doing your research, your goal is to see:
  ➢ How well are those books selling in your genre?
  ➢ Determine whether this is a market you can should tap into

Start by visiting a few (major and independent) bookstores. Take your notebook and a pen and jot down some titles you see in your genre and feature your book topic. Don't be discouraged if you see a ton of books based on the topic you plan to write. That's a good thing. It means it is a popular and sellable topic. For example, publishers bring out dozens of diet books each year, right before the holidays and the summer, and there's still room for yours as well.

Aim to find at least three to five points of difference from their book and yours. This doesn't mean that you have to create all new information. In fact, presenting entirely new information is impossible.

Sticking with our diet book example, the only tried and true way to lose weight is to eat well and work out. Yet authors of diets books have presented this formula in various ways to their readers. Keep this in mind there is no new book topic out there.

A reader is buying your book because of the way you present that information to them. They picked your book over the others because they enjoy reading your point of view and how you voice those views. Therefore, it's how you present the material that counts. If you can show readers a new diet plan and you can prove your method works, you got a hot seller on your hands.

You can continue conducting research by visiting your local library and ask the librarian for *Books in Prints (BIP)*. This is a multi-volume set of reference books, which lists all the books currently available by author, subject, and title. Your library may have the books, or it may have the BIP in digital form. If your library's BIP is digital, get a printout of all the books in your subject area.

Again, don't faint if you see an ultra-lengthy list of books. If there are a lot of books about your book topic, it means this subject is popular. This is a good thing! Matter of fact, if you decide to write a book, and while doing the research you realize that you can't find another book written on the same topic, I would worry. It probably means that other authors have discovered that that particular book topic isn't sellable. Also, check out *Forthcoming* by BIP. It lists all those books which will be released in the next six months.

You'll want to have the books which are the main competition for your book on hand if possible. You don't have to buy them all. You can borrow them from the library, or if they're listed on Amazon.com, you can use Amazon's clever "Look Inside" technology, so you can scan the contents pages of competing titles. Speaking of which, Amazon is your next port of call. Type the subject of your book into the search query box, and you'll get a list of all those books, which touch on your subject area. Print out this list. Having the list handy helps you when the time comes to pick a title. Also, read the descriptions, and all the reviews of any books, which sound as if they might be similar to yours.

RESEARCHING YOUR AUDIENCE

Studying your audience is an important writing and marketing tool. Knowing who your readers are will guide you through the writing phase of your book. For example, if your target audience is single moms, imagine having a dialogue with them as you're writing. Once you complete your book, use the research you gather beforehand to market to your target audience. When researching your audience, use search engines like Google or Bing to find out more information about them. Once you complete your book, use the research you gather beforehand to market to your target audience.

When researching your target audience:

Think about what problems they face and how your book will solve that problem.

Ask yourself if they spend time online. Don't assume everyone is using the internet.

- ➤ What is their demographics?
- ➤ Where do they like to hang out?
- ➤ What are their spending habits?
- ➤ Do they prefer printed books, e-books, or audio books?

Visit sites like the US Census and FedStats.gov to help gather data about your audience

Using the example of working moms again, conduct an online search for 'busy moms diet trend,' 'health concerns of busy moms,' and 'best places for busy moms to work out.' Begin reading magazines, articles, and other periodicals that cater to your audience. Also find specific demographic about your audience by visiting www.fedstat.gov.

Create an avid fan. Someone that would follow you on social media sites, attends your workshops, and pre-ordered your book months in advance. By taking a few minutes to complete the assignment, you now have an idea who your book is speaking to.

Name:

Age:

Ethnicity:

City/State:

Sex:

Marital Status:

Single

Dating

Serious Relationship

Married

Divorced

Widowed

Do they have children? And if so, how many?

Financial Status:

Career:

Hobbies:

Are they on:
Twitter
Facebook
LinkedIn
Pinterest
Other:
Reading Preference:
E-books
Printed books
Audio-books
All of the Above
Do they shop online (circle one): Yes   No

What problems are they facing (i.e. need to lose weight, loss of a loved one)?

How will your book address these problems?

Pretend that your imaginary fan wrote a stellar review for your book and posted it on your Amazon.com book page. Write their book review and include in it their profile:

Additional Notes:

RESEARCH YOUR TARGET AUDIENCE CHECKLIST

- ✓ Gender (Male/Female/Mixed)
- ✓ Age Group
- ✓ Ethnicity
- ✓ Marital Status
- ✓ Location
- ✓ Work/Career
- ✓ Income
- ✓ Social Organizations, Groups, and Associations
- ✓ Religion
- ✓ Political Belief
- ✓ Hobbies and Interest
- ✓ Who do they admire (Public Figures, Celebrities, Motivational Coaches, Pastors, Inspirational Speakers)?

☞☞ Think about what problems they face and how your book will solve that problem

☞☞ Ask yourself if they spend time online. Don't assume everyone is using the Internet

☞☞ What are their demographics

☞☞ Where do they like to hang out?

☞☞ What are their spending habits?

☞☞ Do they prefer printed books, e-books, or audio books?

☞☞ Visit sites like the US Census and FedStats.gov to help gather data about your audience

Become a Storyteller

One of the reasons *Chicken Soup for the Soul* became so popular is because of the stories that touched their reader's heart. They were inspirational, thought-provoking, and entertaining. After a while, a book filled with just facts and figures will bore your readers.

Your book will be more memorable and easier to read if you add personal stories and testimonies throughout the book. Aim to include a story in at least three chapters in your book. The story doesn't have to be an epic novel. Instead, write snippets or tales that outline the topic you're discussing in that chapter. The story could be as short as a couple of paragraph or a few pages. It can also be a standalone section within the chapter or used as a nice transition to go from one topic to another. Types of Stories to include:

- Client Testimonials

- Personal Experiences
Case Studies

Think of several stories that will help you illustrate the topic in your books. Write a brief sentence describing the story. Expand the sentences into one to five paragraphs. Use the sentence you have written in this section as a reference while writing your book.

Chapter 1:

_____

_____

_____

Chapter 2:

_____

_____

_____

Chapter 3:

_____

_____

_____

Chapter 4:

_____

_____

_____

Chapter 5:

_____

_____

_____

Chapter 6:

_____

_____

_____

Chapter 7:

_____

_____

Chapter 8:

_____

_____

Chapter 9:

_____

_____

_____

Chapter 10:

_____

_____

Chapter 11:

_____

_____

Chapter 12:

_____

_____

_____

How to Get Permission to Use Quotes, Articles and Pictures for Your Book

Whenever you use someone else's words, whether you credit them or not, you need to obtain prior permission from either the author or person in charge of the author's estate.

Remember this year: 1923.

That is an industry cutoff date that the book industry used when trying to figure out if an author's work is copyrighted.

As a general rule, anything published before 1923 is considered public domain and copyright laws do not apply.
Technically, anything 60+ years after the author's death is free to use since that's when the copyright expires. But, seriously, do you really want to get involved with the sticky logistics of that?

At this point, I should make it extremely clear that I'm not an attorney, so always check with a lawyer before publishing your work. Because, if you use someone words without permission, you may be held liable. Just imagine what a lawsuit would do to your creditability AND your bank account.

Also, it doesn't matter if you're self-published or not. All publishing companies publish your book under the assumption *you* sought all necessary permission *prior* to publication which is stipulated in your contract. So basically, if the stuff hits the fan, you're on your own.

Fact Check: Whether you use a quote, statistic, interview, or theory, you must fact check your information to make sure it's accurate. You can do this by conducting an extensive Google search to locate the original origin of the information or do it "old school" by checking old magazines, journals, and books references. You can also seek the help of a reference librarian. Once you checked the information, write down the author and any contact information you can find.

Ask Permission: Once you find the source, write the content owner an email asking for permission to use the quote, excerpt, interview, etc... In the letter, include your name, your book title, and the exact information you want to include in your book.

Follow-up: After 7-10 days, if you haven't received a response, send a short follow-up e-mail. If you still haven't received a response, you can continue to follow-up or try to find new contact information for that person and start over. Your persistence will really depend on how much you want their information in your book.

Additional Tips

- ✓ Don't be surprised if the content owner gives you permission to use the information for a fee. This is not unusual, and again, you have to decide on how much you want that quote or article in your book.

- ✓ To give you a specific cut-off date to work with, anything published before 1923 is considered public domain and copyright laws do not apply. Some examples are works by Mark Twain, Jane Austin, and Shakespeare.

- ✓ Make sure you receive written permission and keep a hard copy of the letter in your files for future reference. If you're crunch on time, seek out quotes that are over 100 years old. When you're on a deadline and need to get your book to your editor or printer, Shakespeare is going to become your best friend.

- ✓ You need permission to use photos in your book as well. However, you can purchase the right to use a photo from such sites as Dreamstime.com.

- ✓ Visit Article Submissions sites like EzineArticle.com for articles you can use for free. However, you must not alter or change the information in any way and are required to use the full article in it entirely. Also, make sure to include the author information as well.

PLR stands for Private Label Rights, and are already created content (eBooks, reports, video, audio, etc…) you can purchase and use in just about any way you can imagine. Using PLR content is a tricky thing because of the "ick factor" many associate with it.

In essence, you're purchasing the right to use content and claim it as your own. But isn't hiring a ghostwriter basically the same idea? Well, sorta, not really.

When you hire a ghostwriter, you are:
a) sharing your knowledge and expertise with the ghostwriter who will transfer your ideas and put it in print; and
b) it's your exclusive content, which means no one else has the right to use the content in your book unless you give them permission to do so.

With PLRs anyone with the means can purchase the right to use the same content you purchase.

If you do decide to use PLRs, consider ways that you can incorporate it into your book and products that will make it uniquely your own.

Expand and rewrite paragraphs, only use a small section from a PLR report, or offer the PLR as a bonus content for your readers. I don't recommend you add your name to PLR content unless you add value to it in some way.

Once purchased, PLRs (Private Label Rights) are yours to use, however you like, and can help supplement your book.

And I can't say this enough: when in doubt, talk to a lawyer!

Create a Writing Schedule

First, I want you to take an honest assessment on how you spend your time. When I say honest, I mean honest. Write down what you do from the time you wake up until the time you go to bed. That doesn't mean I want you to write down every millisecond of your day. Instead, create a timeline that you generally follow. Especially, include the times when you focus on one task such as watching TV from 8-10 p.m. or checking your Facebook page as soon as you start work. (Yes, I noticed you update your Facebook status while you were at your 9-5 but I won't snitch on you.)

TV along with Facebook and other social media sites is what I like to call Time Vampires.

Time Vampire are activities you do that make times fly, and before you know it, you just wasted an hour checking your Facebook newsfeed when you could have been doing something more constructive, like… writing your book.

When reviewing your daily schedule, eliminate the Time Vampires. Now, you have freed up time during your day to write your book.

Also, schedule your writing during the times when you feel most creative. Maybe you're an early bird and decide to wake up at 4 a.m. so you can write for a few hours before you head off to work.

For me, I eventually discovered I'm at my most creative from 10 p.m. to 2 o'clock in the morning. (No kidding—I'm re-reading this chapter and laughing at myself because it's now 2:46 a.m.) Why? It could be because the house is at its quietest. The phone is not ringing; I don't have any errands to run; I'm not constantly checking the time because I have a meeting with a client coming up; or worrying about getting my client's project completed. Whatever the reason, from 10 p.m. on is when my muse decides to pay me a visit, and you don't want to miss a visit from your muse.

Despite what writing schedule you create, stick to it, and make sure your family is aware of it as well. If you decide to write at 7 p.m. when your household is at its busiest, your family need to be aware that for the next hour or so, you're not to be disturb. Also, turn off your phones, TVs, and unless you're doing research for your book, the Internet. Yes, your computer works without the Internet, and if you don't have access to Time Vampires like YouTube, Facebook, and Twitter, you won't be easily distracted.

When creating a writing schedule, ideally, you want to write during the time:

☞☞ When you're at your most creative

☞☞ When you can avoid the most distractions

Add this time to your calendar or daily agenda. Better yet, add it to your to-do list, program the time on your phone so you can receive a daily reminder, tell your writing buddy (more about writing buddies in an upcoming chapters) to call you 15 minutes before to remind you to write. Do what you have to do to make sure you write during the time you commit to.

Also, include the amount of words, or word count, you plan to write during that time. Give yourself a goal and write until you reach completion. However, feel free to adjust your word count goal to fit into the time you allotted for writing. For example, I consider myself a fast typist, yet writing 1000 words in 15 minutes is beyond my skill level at this time.

	Mon	Tue	Wed	Thur	Fri
Word Count					
Hours					

Dealing with (Writer's (Road) Block

Let me first start by saying that I don't believe in writer's block per se, mainly because I never experience it. However, I have experienced writer's distractions, writer's procrastinations, and writers WTF am I supposed to do with this character now!

In essence, I consider writer's block as roadblock we, writers, face from time to time.

Some examples of writing road block:

☛☛Distractions

☞☞Not sure where to take your characters or storyline

☞☞Procrastinations

☞☞Unclear ideas

☞☞Unorganized book format

☞☞Not sure how to expand on a topic in a chapter

So how do you remove writer's roadblock? Well, for me, I find starting from the beginning of the book—yes, the very beginning—and reading the book to the section where I was stuck does the trick. While I'm re-reading my book, I begin to remember what message I was trying to convey, tend to tweak things as I go along and by the time I reach the last sentence, I'm back in the writing zone.

To offer you more tricks to remove writing blocks out of your path, I asked my mastermind group, Write Your Book in 30 Days! to share their tips with you. Below is an excerpt from that Facebook conversation.

Just Write That
Book Already!

 Don Miskel Whenever I get writer's block (which I've pretty much trained myself NOT to get), I just write something else. This is why I always have side projects and unfinished concepts that can become entirely different stories. If you get stuck, take a break, wrap your head around something else and when the "blockage" has cleared, resume your primary project.

September 4 at 7:54pm · Like · 👍 1

 Author Stephanie White I write poetry or a magazine article to keep me focused and out of that grey area of writer's block

September 4 at 8:06pm · Like · 👍 1

 K Lynn Brown Step away from the writing project for a day maybe 2. If on a tight deadline watch movies that fit genre of writing. I write dramatic fiction m romance . A quality or favorite love story motivates and gets creative juices flowing. Works for me.

 Veronica Blakely When you have writer's block; don't try and force words onto the page as that will frustrate you more. Taking a walk always calm me down and get my creative juices flowing. I make sure to have my digital recorder w/ me to capture whatever idea comes to mind. Note: do not get on your cell phone texting/talking because this will only interrupt the process. If you can't take a walk, move away from that writing space just to have a change of scenery.

Something else I do is brainstorm by creating a list of what I want to write about, then I make an outline and start writing. That process can take place within a day, a week, or a month. This will at least give you a starting point. Hope this helps and Joy you are welcomed to use my comments.

Friday at 7:39am · Unlike · 👍 3

Having the plan to deal with distractions can help you stay on your writing course. The fact is, life happens. Kids want your attention; the car needs a tune-up; coaching clients need emergency support. All of these things and more will eat into your writing time if you're not aware of them

As bad as distractions are, procrastination is the real killer. When you're writing a book and get stuck, suddenly it seems much more important to finish watching season 7 of your favorite TV show, braid your hair, or even redesign your website. Anything is better than sitting down to write.

And when you combine the possibility of procrastination with some of life's distractions…well, you can see how it might take you several years to finally get that book written. So how do prevent this from happening?

Have a distraction-free plan, ready to go.

Obviously, you can't plan for the unexpected life hiccups, but you can (and should) plan ahead for things like your kids and pets and coaching clients.

Schedule play dates during your writing time. So, while your kids are having fun playing at their friend's house, you have a quiet home to write in. It's a win-win.

Close your office door and place a "Do Not Disturb" sign on the door.

Post your business hours on your website and let clients know you will not be responding to email or phone calls except during office hours.

Turn off your phone, email, and Skype during writing time.

Use a software program such as Scrivener which offers a full screen, distraction free, writing environment.

And again, turn off your internet access during your writing time.

Procrastination is a little tougher to deal with, because it's all on you. The key is to know what's likely to trigger your procrastination and design ways to keep yourself motivated.

Some ideas include:

Rewarding yourself with a favorite treat or trip to the spa after a week of writing.

Enlist the help of an accountability partner to keep you on track.

Make a commitment to do something unpleasant (such as making a donation to a political candidate you don't support) if you don't reach your weekly writing goals.

EXERCISE: BRAINSTORM POTENTIAL DISTRACTIONS AND WRITE A PLAN TO DEAL WITH THEM.

Distraction	Plan

EXERCISE: RECOGNIZE WHEN YOU'RE MOST LIKELY TO PROCRASTINATE, AND DECIDE NOW HOW YOU'LL RESIST THE URGE.

Writing Milestone

Walter Arthur Ward was quoted as saying, "If you can dream it, you can achieve it." There something to writing and visualizing your goal that just works. For instance, studies show that athletes who use mental imagery during training to help improve their performance increase their performance in comparison to those who train without using visualization practices.

Writing down each milestone is an excellent way to help you stay on track during the book process. Milestone checkpoints are small tasks or assignment with a specific period that will help you reach your major goal. For instance, instead of saying, "I want to write 10 chapters of my book," your milestone statements may be:

By the end of the day, I will write 500 words

I will have 3 chapters completed by May 31

I will have 10,000 words by July 30

Milestones are created based on your overall plans for your book such as:

- The day you want the book completed
- The day you want to seek out a book agent or begin the self-publishing process
- The day you want to begin showing your books to your colleagues for peer reviews
- The day you need to send your book to the editor, printer, or interior book designer

Set a major goal

Next, write the date you would like to reach your goal.

Once you have an end date in mind, write all the steps you need to complete to reach your goal. Don't worry about the exact order. Instead, focus on the tasks needed to reach your major goal.

Next, arrange the steps you've written into a timeline from beginning to end. These are your writing milestones.

Once you complete each task, you'll know you're one step closer to reaching your goal and finishing your book.

Going back to the original example, if you wanted to write 10 chapters of your books in 3 months and you expect each chapter to take at least 10 days to complete, you would set a date to complete each chapter based on this timeline.

How you keep track of your milestones will be based on your personal style. Maybe you prefer to jot everything down on a to-do list and cross them off as you accomplish them or maybe you like to use a large bulletin board and place your milestones on postcards and take them off the board as you complete them. Your system could involve using a wall calendar or a project management software. Personally, I love www.myintervals.com. They offer a free trial, and you can plot out your book project using their easy-to-use task tool. The best part—they send you daily remainders of the tasks you still haven't completed.

Despite what system you use, keeping track of your goals and milestones will help you stay motivated to write your book.

Use the worksheet on the following pages to create your own writing milestones. When creating your milestones, consider creating at least 5-7 goals but no more than 10. Anything over 10 may become overwhelming and discourage you from finishing your book. Once you have them listed, I want you to treat your milestones as your affirmations: read them out loud and visualize yourself completing the task daily.

MY WRITING MILESTONES

To reach my goal, I need to reach the following milestones by a specific date.

These milestones are:

Milestone #1:

_____

_____

_____

_____

_____

_____

_____

_____

Date to be completed:

_____

Milestone #2:

_____

_____

_____

_____

_____

_____

_____

_____

_____

Date   to   be   completed:

_____

Milestone #3:

_____

_____

_____

_____

_____

_____

_____

_____

_____

Date   to   be   completed:

_____

Milestone #4:

_____

_____

_____

_____

_____

_____

_____

_____

Date   to   be   completed:

_____

Milestone #5:

_____

_____

_____

_____

_____

_____

_____

_____

_____

Date   to   be   completed:

_____

Find a Writing Buddy

A writing buddy is your success partner. They will help you stay on track while you're aiming to reach your goal. Hopefully the person you select to be your writing buddy will either be writing a book at the same time as you or has written a book previously. I hope that the person you decide to work with can help you kick your writing into high gear. Your writing buddy's job is to make sure you stay on track with your writing milestones, and your job is to do the same for them.

I recommend that you find a writing buddy with the same mindset as you. When you make a conscientious effort to work with someone, always aim upward by beginning to associate with people whose goals, dreams and aspirations align with you. Using the Internet is an excellent way to connect with people who have similar goals as your own.

Consider using social media to find your writing buddy. For instance, you can post a status on Facebook saying something along the lines of "I'm looking for a writing buddy, inbox me." Even better, join a writing group by checking out Meetup.com or Googling the term "writing group" and inserting the area where you live in the search box.

I would treat the selection of finding a writing buddy like a job interview because the person you work with is supposed to be a positive influence in your life. Why would you select someone who constantly says (or tweets): "I collect haters" or "Why do these things always happen to me?"

That's not the type of person you want to associate with because that's a clear indication they don't have the right mindset to get things done, and it's hard to continuously work with someone who focuses solely on the negative. I know how Hippie this sounds, but negative people have a tendency to bring your energy down. If you begin to associate with someone with plenty of 'baggage' or 'drama,' all those negative vibes begin to attach themselves to you.

Also, find someone who has an entrepreneur mindset. I don't necessarily mean they must have a business, or they are entrepreneurs, but someone who understands a book as a business—because it is. Whether you're writing a fiction book or a nonfiction book, the end goal is to sell your book and hopefully make a profit.

The job of a Writing Buddy is to keep you on track with your writing goals by becoming your Accountability Partner, and it's your job to do the same for them.

Check in with your buddy regularly based on your schedule and try to stick to that schedule as much as possible. If you two agree to talk every Saturday at 4 p.m., be mindful that your buddy rearranged their schedule to be available at that time. If you can't make the call or meet them in person at that time, as a courtesy, try to at least let them know before time, and ask them to do the same for you. You can communicate with your buddy using:

☞☞Skype

☞☞Phone

☞☞In person meetings

☞☞Text

☞☞E-mail

☞☞Instant Message

No matter how you decide to check-in with your writing buddy, keep it short and simple. For instance, if you call your buddy every week, limit the call to about 20 minutes because you don't want to side-track from your writing schedule.

During each meeting (whether by phone, in person, or on Skype):

☞☞ Discuss your previous writing milestones and what goals you completed so far with your writing buddy

☞☞ Also discuss the challenges you face during the week and the progress you made so far

☞☞ Mention any success story you want to share

☞☞ Set goals (your writing milestones) for the following weeks

Also plan to have at least three intensive writing sessions (during the beginning, middle, and end phase of the book process), and spend at least 2-4 hours together discussing each other book.

These writing sessions can be broken down as follows:

1.   Begin by discussing your current writing goals and planned milestones

2.   Have your buddy read at least 1-3 chapters of your manuscript or if you haven't written anything yet, the planned outline of your book. If working with someone not in your area, send him or her the information before the phone call so he or she can read it before time. If you're meeting in person, make sure to have a hard copy of your chapters available.

3.   Receive constructive feedback from your writing buddy regarding your work so far and return the favor.

4.   Discuss how you can make your book better to meet the needs of your audience.

What information is missing?

☞☞What information can be removed?

☞☞What questions are you not answering for your reader?

☞☞Is the topic/niche/problem clearly defined?

☞☞Are you writing in a clear and concise matter (In other words, are you providing the necessary information and avoiding the fluff)?

5. Discuss your next writing milestones

6. Begin reworking your chapters based on their feedback or start the next section in your book

Keep your buddy on the phone (or online) with you during the entire writing session and use the mute button when you're not talking to each other if you have background noise in your area. You will be amazed how much work you'll finish when you have someone working on their book the same exact time you are working on yours. If you don't have free long distance on your home or cell phone, I recommend using Skype. Even if you don't have a webcam (or your camera shy), you can use the microphone and speaker on your computer to make a Skype call. If you're meeting in person, consider meeting at a library or find a location like one that offers free Wi-Fi. Barnes and Noble and Panera Bread encourage their customers to hang out for as long as they like.

GETTING STARTED

- Print out your manuscript
- Read it from beginning to end with little interruptions
- Cut out any content that doesn't fit or add to your book
- Add any data and content you feel is lacking
- Check for Chapter Coherency
- Does the content in your chapters make sense with the topic you're discussing?
- Would it work better in another section of your book?
- Did you add transitions throughout the chapters, especially in the end?
- Add your voice and personal spin in your manuscript if you haven't done so already
- Check for any grammar errors, typos, word usage, and other mistakes so you can have the cleanest version of your manuscript possible to share with others. Consider hiring an editor—especially if you plan to self-publish your book

The process of reading and revising your book is so you can get a sense of how the material reads. When you've finished this initial read-through, ask yourself whether what you've written stays close to your book blurb. If it doesn't, either you can change your blurb—perhaps you've been inspired with some creative new ideas—or you can change some chapters in your books to complement your initial ideas better.

While this read-through is fresh in your mind, now is the time to take action and revise your book where needed. Have you covered most of what you want to include? What else do you think the book needs?

Before you begin making changes, rename your document (booktitle_1, booktitle_ B, B1, or whatever name filing process you decide to use). Now go through your manuscript and take out the material you've decided you want to eliminate. If it's too painful to hit the Delete key, cut the material and paste it into another document.

In this read-through, add the material your book needs. For instance, perhaps you've done some additional research. Read your manuscript through to check for coherency. Also make sure that you've included transitions at the end of each chapter.

In addition, as you're reading through the material, considering how you jazz up the content. Maybe there's a story you want to share with your readers that you know will drive the topic home.

Or perhaps you would like to include a reference guide to make it easier for your readers to find the information you mentioned throughout your book.

Finally check for grammar and word usage to create, what calls, a clean version of your book.

Creating Your Book Team

Writing your book is the easy part. I know, I know, it doesn't seem that way now while you're in the midst of it all. But it's true.

At this very moment, you have the most control you will ever have over your book. You don't have to deal with bookstore owners, come up with marketing plans, seek out interviews and book reviews, or worry about someone— anyone—buying your book. Right now you are experiencing the calm before the storm.

But it's time to kick things up a notch and begin thinking about the next phase of the book process. So, it's time to talk about your Book Team. Your Book Team are the people you will hire to help you with the writing, marketing, and publishing of your book(s).

Your Book Team May Include:
- Editor
- Web Site Designer
- Interior Book Layout Design
- Typesetter
- Book Cover Designer
- Copywriter (for your bio, synopsis, and sale sheets)
- Indexer
- Photographer
- Intellectual Property Attorney
- Marketing Consultant
- Publicist
- Book Coach

In my opinion, you:

- Should hire an editor.
- Should hire a book cover designer.
- Can learn how to do the interior book layout, but need the software or a great template to do it right. So, it's better to hire a professional.
- Can learn how to create a website using WordPress. But, hire a professional if you need major assistance with setting up the site.
- Should consult with an IP (Intellectual Property) lawyer, at least once.
- Should hire a Book Coach.
- Should only hire a Publicist if it's within your budget.

Conclusion

Just Write That Book Already! was written as a labor of love. I wrote this book as a tool for those who want to write a book but, for whatever reason, are stuck in a story of why they can't write one. By working through the activities in the book, I hope you have released those stories that have been holding you back.

If you stumble along the way, remind yourself why you wanted to write a book in the first place, pick yourself up and keep going. Even if you only write a page every other day or write a chapter every month, by the end of the year, you'd have completed your book. So keep going. Keep Writing.

If you are looking for a one-on-one assistant and personal guidance, I'm here for you. I am also offering group sessions, virtual workshops, teleclasses, and host group goal-setting projects for those that work well with working with a strict deadline while working within a supportive group setting.

Visit my website at www.litdiva.com or email me at joy@litdiva.com to get in touch with me. I hope to hear from you in the near future.

Joy Farrington
Joy the Lit Diva

Follow me across all Social Media Platforms
@JoytheLitDiva
www.twitter.com/JoytheLitDiva
www.facebook.com/JoytheLitDiva
www.instagram.com/JoytheLitDiva
www.periscope.tv/JoytheLitDiva
www.youtube.com/JoytheLitDiva

Below is an edited excerpt from the transcript of a teleconference I had based on my Just Write Your Book Already! (Formally known as Write That Book Already!) workshop. I wanted to include the Q&A Session in this book because I feel the questions that were asked by the participants may be useful, as they may be questions you have as well.

Joy Farrington: I want to go ahead and open up the lines to see if anybody has any questions. We also have some questions from Facebook that I'm going to answer as well. Okay, so the lines are unmuted. There is plenty of noise in the background; you may want to mute your phone. Anybody who has questions, you can go ahead.

Linda: I have a question.

Joy Farrington: Ok. Go ahead with your question.

Linda: Hi, Linda from Detroit. So this is my question. Say my writing goal is for an hour a day. Is that just straight writing? How do you calculate the time for research or does research fall into that writing hour or that writing two hours?

Joy Farrington: No, Writing. We've done the research. So if your writing goal is one hour a day, that's just the writing.

Linda: Okay, so no more research?

Joy Farrington: Yeah, so you have to find time to research your stuff. So you may spend an hour to half an hour each.

Linda: Okay

Joy Farrington: I have a question from Alana. She posted a question on Facebook... "Getting advisers, an assistant when your topic is either difficult, or it's in a subject area that already has set the lead among its followers." I would say to that, that you would be surprised how many people are out there that are. If you post online and let them know that "I have a goal in mind. I have a book. The topic is somewhat difficult but I have a book, and I want your help with it," and you post this, I mean, Twitter and Facebook, it's global; so if you post a comment like that on there, you're going to get the help that you need.

To get an adviser and assistant on a topic is not difficult actually. Just post a request or send a mass e-mail to your list or on Facebook or Twitter and let everybody know what your goal is, what your book project is and just ask for help.

I have Janet Cath.; she wanted "tips on finding a good collaborative partner/editor when writing an autobiography." Again, just ask. If you're in a writing group, you could just ask everybody, "What can I do? I have an autobiography; would anybody be interested in writing it with me?" If you're on Facebook, put up a status update, "I have an autobiography. Would anybody be interested in co-authoring with me?" Maybe you'll find somebody that you kind of like what they are saying on their status; then just go ahead and contact them.

Anybody on the call has another question?

Dianne: I have a question. I just went to Facebook, and I didn't see your writers group. Could you give that site again?

Joy Farrington: It's Write Your Book in 30 Days! You can do a Facebook search or type in your browser www.facebook.com/groups/bookin30

Dianne: Okay.

Joy Farrington: Is that you, Dianne?

Dianne: Yes, you recognized my voice.

Joy Farrington: Yeap! Okay, I have a question on chat. "I have an outline for my book and I start to write, but I'm getting stuck on writing past 100 pages. Any suggestions?"

I would say take the time off from writing and read what you already wrote. You could start back from the beginning and read, then by the time you reach page 100, maybe that will help you figure out what you want to write, or you could take what you already wrote, give it to somebody that's familiar with your topic and let them read it, then ask them what's missing. But 100 pages, that's a good start. You're almost done, so don't give up even if maybe you're not writing right now. Maybe you're spending most of your time researching instead, but don't give up on what you're doing.

Denise Carol: I have a question.

Joy Farrington: Go ahead.

Denise Carol: My name is Denise Carol. Once I finish my book, how do I get it published?

Joy Farrington: Are you thinking about self-publishing?

Denise Carol: I'm not sure. I've never written a book, so I have no knowledge about self-publishing or even going to a publisher. What are my options? What should I do?

Joy Farrington: Basically, you only have two options: either you go to a publisher, or you could just publish the book yourself. If you're going to a publisher, the steps would include finding an agent, writing a query letter.

Actually, writing a query letter, then sending the letter to an agent. The agent will contact the publishing companies on your behalf then you two go through the negotiation process. That process could take about 1-3 years, from the time of finding an agent up to the time it takes to get your book published. Even if you find an agent today and sign a contract, a publishing company won't publish your book for about a year. Now, if you self-publish books, the process is: who do you publish with? Who will be the printer for the manuscript? For print on demand, I recommend Createspace (www.createspace.com) For a printer, you have 48-Hours Book (www.48hoursbook.com), and you also have Lighting Source (www.lightingsource.com). Because you're printing it yourself, there is no waiting period. Once your book is done, once it's edited, and if you don't have a book designer, you typeset it yourself. You can use the template on Createspace. Then your book is published. So it depends. You have more involvement if you're a self-published author.

Denise Carol: Okay. But do you also have to market it yourself if you're self-published?

Joy Farrington: But it doesn't matter if you publish the book yourself, or you get published.

You're marketing the book yourself. Many people don't realize it.

Denise Carrol: How do you sell it? How do you sell the book?

Joy Farrington: You have to ask yourself how you're planning to sell the book. So if you're selling the book in bookstores, if that's your primary goal, get your book in bookstores, then you have to get a distributor, then once you have a distributor, you're more than likely. Again, this is if you self-publish. You're going to have to contact the bookstore and let them know that your book is available and ask them if they could put it in the bookstores. It's easier to get in the bookstores if you're a published author (with a major publisher) but either way, you're going to do plenty of marketing yourself. If you're selling it online, online would be a lot easier than bookstores because you have more control of it. You could have it on your website, promote it to online book clubs. If you just type in book clubs, you'd be surprised how many websites will come up. Many book clubs have their own website, and you could contact those book clubs individually. You just say, "I have a book. This is what it's about. I'd love to talk to your book club about it," and go from there.

There are several avenues you can use. It really depends on what your target is. I will set a couple of goals of your market. Again, if your goal is book clubs or bookstores, that's going to be another set of goals that you have to reach. If your goal is a book club, selling it to book clubs, that's a different set of goals you have to reach. It really depends on where you want to go.

Denise Carrol: You just answered the majority of my questions. I have completed manuscript; I have two. I have a children's book I completed, and I have a fiction manuscript I completed. I have an article published in a local magazine in Baltimore, Maryland. These magazines are in the library, so they are free magazines, but it was just an essay that I wrote in October concerning ghost stories. It wasn't fiction. It was supposed to have been based on something in your life, and you used that as a springboard to write this essay, which I did. I consider myself a published author; however, everyone who I submit my manuscript to, they love it, they like it, but then again, it comes with the fees. I'm trying to see what would be considered a fair amount for someone who has never published a fiction book as far as financial arise. I've been offered all different kinds of deals. I talked to people and talked to publishing companies, they have offered me different deals. I have talked to _____. Have you ever heard of that yet?

Joy Farrington: Okay, let me stop you for a second. When you say fees, do you mean the fees you're paying them or the fees they are paying you?

Denise Carrol: No the fees that they want me to pay them.

Joy Farrington: Okay, but then: they are not publishing your book? You're paying them to publish your book?

Denise Carrol: I'm paying them to publish my book.

Joy Farrington: Right, like Random House, you will not give Random House a dollar to publish your book. They will pay you to publish your book. They are not a publisher. What you're talking about is vanity press.

Denise Carol: How do you...? Can I contact them? What do I do?

Joy Farrington: Well, to contact them, you're going to need an agent. They really like talking to agents.

Denise Carol: Okay, so basically if you get an agent, then I wouldn't have to pay upfront?

Joy Farrington: Wait, there's two questions in that. I want to address the vanity press because I'm a little worried about that. If you get an agent, they are going to do the negotiations for you. Most agents have law degrees, so they know contracts and all that stuff. A good agent will tell you, "This is a good deal. This is a bad deal. Maybe we should hold out for this." That's what the agent's job is. You could also contact published authors and ask them. "I am self-published. I just want to ask quick questions: Do you think this sounds good to you?" Just ask them a quick question. Don't take too much of their time. For the vanity press, I'm a little worried about that because vanity press will take all your money and you have a book you cannot sell. The reason that you can't sell the book is that you have to price it so high, no one wants to buy it. So if you're going to go that route, you might as well publish your book yourself. (Use) Createspace to publish a book. You can print a book between $2 and $4; it really depends on how big your book is.

Denise Carol: So CreateSpace?

Joy Farrington: Yes, Createspace is (through) Amazon. Let's say your book is 100 pages, and Createspace charges you $2.50 to print that one book and you priced the book at $10. You have a $7.50 profit right there, whereas if you go to the vanity press, with the vanity press, you have to charge about $30 just to make that same sum of money. Because they price the book so high that you really have no other choice because vanity presses, they are notorious for taking author's money. That's how they do business. They don't make money selling your book. They make money from publishing your books. Do you understand the difference?

Denise Carol: Yes

Joy Farrington: Okay, so I wouldn't. If anybody comes to you and says, "I will publish your book. Your book is wonderful. We want to be your publisher, but there's a fee," that's a vanity press.

Denise Carol: That's a big fee. I mean, a book is like thousands.

Joy Farrington: Yeah, that's crazy. You go publish your book yourself for free. I'm not exaggerating. You could publish it for free. Go on to Createspace; you could submit your book for free. You could create your cover for free.

Everything's for free. There's no reason to spend thousands of dollars.

Denise Carol: Okay, but I do need someone to edit, right?

Joy Farrington: Yes, you definitely need an editor. Now the editor could start between 6-15 cents a word. It depends on the editor or the type of editor that you get, but you're definitely going to want an editor. Besides the editing, you'll need to buy an ISBN. If you do not want to buy ISBN, I recommend it, but you just do not have the money for it, you can get a free ISBN at Create Space. If you don't have the money; will issue one for you. You could use it—the cover designer (On) Create Space—and you can make a decent book cover for yourself. Their tools have actually gotten a lot better over the years, so you could really create a fine book cover for yourself. So don't spend thousands of dollars on a vanity press when with a little elbow grease, you could do some things yourself.

Art Garfield: Can anybody hear me?

Joy Farrington: We can hear you; go ahead.

Art Garfield: I like the information you just stated, and how long is this seminar over? Is it over now? Because I just joined in like 15 minutes ago.

Joy Farrington: Yeah; technically, it's over. It says 7 o'clock, but I'm going to stay on a few minutes to answer everybody's questions. Do you have a question for me?

Art Garfield: Sure, I do. This is Art Garfield.

Joy Farrington: Hi, Art!

Art Garfield: My question is, if you use Create Space to publish your book, now going to somebody like a major publisher, Random House or whoever, when they publish your book, they actually get behind it with their promotional team, right? That's what they bring to the table, of course, right?

Joy Farrington: Right.

Art Garfield: And if you use Create Space, you're basically your own promotional team. You're doing it yourself.

Joy Farrington: Right, but I want to be honest with you. People don't realize Random House, St. Martin's…Unless you're on a Twilight or Hunger Games level, you'll be surprised how much they are really doing. They will write up the press release for you. They are on the distribution list, so it's easier to get to bookstores, and bookstores are more likely to place your book in the bookstore, but they are really not doing what you think they are going to do like when you're with a publisher. You think you're going to get your billboard; you're going to get the full page ad in the magazines. That's what you expect, but unless they feel they are going to make plenty of money from you and from your book, they are not going to put that extra effort in. Especially nowadays where printed books aren't selling as they used to. Everybody is more about e-books than books. For publishers like Random House, St. Martin, and so forth, I believe the statistics are they concentrate their marketing—90% of the marketing—on 1%-5% of their authors, so what does that leave for you? If that's the case, many authors do their marketing themselves regardless if they are a self-published author or a mainstream author. They really have to go out of their way to get this stuff done themselves. It's easier; it's considered more credible if you're with a big publishing house, granted, but you're pretty much going to be doing the same work.

Art Garfield: Here's another question: How many pages is the average book because once you get past 30 pages, you're going like, "Okay, can I sell it now?"

Joy Farrington: Like when you're done, right? I would say the average would be; I won't say average; I'll say decent size. A decent size is about 150 pages. That's going to be 35,000-40,000 words.

Art Garfield: Okay.

Joy Farrington: That's a decent size, a decent size for a printed book, but you can have a book with 80 pages in it; you can have a book with 300 pages in it. There's really no average.

Art Garfield: What about children's books?

Joy Farrington: Children's books, those are going to be 7-20 pages. There are going to be maybe four sentences on each page.

Art Garfield: Where is the best place to get children's books purchased?

Joy Farrington: Do you mean where are children books sold, or to buy?

Art Garfield: To buy

Joy Farrington: Honestly, that's not my forte. I do know there are services out there. There are plenty of services that cater to that. I came across it; I can't think of it like off the top of my head. Actually, I was thinking about writing a children's book when I saw it. What they do is, they give you the drawing. They have to illustrate it for you, and all you do is write the text. I think you paid about $500 for that. I thought that was a really good price because if you hire an illustrator, you're probably going to be spending more than that. Unfortunately, I wish I could remember that website, but maybe you could Google it, like Google children's book publishers or print of demand children's publishers or something like that. You might be able to find it.

Art Garfield: Okay, another question: So it doesn't matter if it's a biography, autobiography, fiction, nonfiction or whatever to determine the page count, right?

Joy Farrington: I wouldn't concentrate so much on the page count, no. I'll concentrate on the content because if you do that, if you start to tell yourself you're going to write a 200-page book but your book ended at page 100, you're going to have plenty of fluff in your book. You're going to lose your readers.

Art Garfield: Right.

Joy Farrington: So I don't want you to do that. If you're looking for a goal, like if you're telling yourself, "Once I reach this goal, I'm going to stick to it," that's one thing, but if you're trying to figure out when you could stop, you stop when your book is done. So if your book is only 30 pages and you don't want to print the book because it's 30 pages, you worry a lot about what people would think, then sell it as an e-book.

Art Garfield: Does page count determine what you price for it?

Joy Farrington: Yes, because the more pages you have, the more it will cost you to print your book, and this sets how much you want to make from that book.

Art Garfield: Aha.

Joy Farrington: Yes. So if you have a point price of $8 per book and your book costs $5 to print, you're going to sell your book for $13, you understand?

Let me say first, I'm sorry, I haven't been able to get to you guys. I see you guys posting; I wasn't able to answer any question. Kim asks, "At what stage do you start thinking about reviews, and how do you get them done? How important is getting reviewed to a book's success?"

A review is important for a book's success. Word of mouth is the best marketing you could have for a book, product, anything that you're selling; word of mouth is the best thing possible. I will get the book review as soon as your book is clean enough to send it out, which means, your book has gone through the editor. It needs to be proofread, but your editor has gone through it. It's clean, you won't be embarrassed if someone sees it, and I will get that book bound, which means it's not loose pages. You can bind it together, and you can send that out to people before the book is even published. So if your publication date is three months from now but your book is ready to be reviewed, you can send it out from now. The sooner, the better because that gives you more leeway, because reviews take about 2-3 months before they start coming back, so once you get that going, you have those reviews coming in, then that's something you could include on your website, those reviews you got during your press kit. You might even be able to put them on that first page. Many books have that testimonial, the "what people are saying" page. You could put the reviews on there. Anybody else on the call?

Art Garfield: I'm so sorry. I have one more question. I'm sorry, this is the last one.

Joy Farrington: Okay, I'm going to hold you to that. (Laughs)

Art Garfield: (Laughs) The question is, my book is about an experience I had as a writer on Cosby's last sitcom. It's the behind the scenes, not exposed, but just my experience. What I mean is, are there any legalities of using his name in the title? I told him I wrote a book and so he didn't say, "Hey, watch it." He didn't say anything like "you better not use my name," but my question to you is, are there any legalities with using his name in the title?

Joy Farrington: First, I'll say I'm not a lawyer, so don't take this as legal advice. I have to say that. So, in that way, you can't sue me but are you using the information about him in your book?

Art Garfield: Yeah.

Joy Farrington: Is it factual?

Art Garfield: It's factual. It's a real book.

Joy Farrington: There might be a problem with slander because he might be cool with it now but he might not be cool with it when it is published, so you definitely need to talk to a lawyer about that. I would contact a copyright lawyer.

Art Garfield: It's not bad. It's a book of plays.

Joy Farrington: No, but still, is his name is going to be in the title?

Art Garfield: My question was, are there any legalities in using his name. Bill Cosby saved my life.

Joy Farrington: You could use his name in the title. It's a name. His name is not copyrighted. I won't use Oprah's name in the title because Oprah is a brand. You see the difference?

Art Garfield: Yeah.

Joy Farrington: But if it's just a name, no, you could go ahead and use that, but I would definitely talk to a lawyer to get his feedback to see what he says because there is that chance of slander. Even if it's just written—an email that the guy sent you that says it's okay. Just have something written so he is aware of what you're doing or you send it to him before time and ask, "Just so you know what I'm writing, so when the time comes that I publish, you're not shocked by it." Just to get the heads up and again, I would go back to the lawyer and just talk to them about the legalities of it first.

Art Garfield: Right. Got you. Alright, that's cool, thank you.

Joy Farrington: Okay, 15 minutes after the hour. I know you guys still have a few questions. What I'm going to do is, I'm going to go ahead and take it, but I do want to answer some questions in the chatroom because you guys are blowing up the chat room and I don't want to forget you guys. Let me scroll through here, grab a question real quick, and this is going to be the last question for tonight.

"Will school systems purchase books?"

Yes, and what you do is, you don't call them books. They are educational materials. Everybody, organizations, nonprofits, school boards, school systems, they have a budget for educational materials, so if you tell them about your books, and it's something that it fits into, like there are group of children, let's say they have a drug-free program, like a huge drug-free program and your book is related to that, so tell them you have educational material to offer them, and then volunteer your time to speak about the topic as well. So they are buying the books as educational materials, but they have you come in and talk about it.

Actually, in this case, it's easier if you're a self-published author than if you're a published author because you're selling your own books, whereas if you're a published author, you have to go through them to buy the books to bring it to the school. That means the school has to buy the books through the publisher. There is a middleman involved.

But use the term educational material. As a matter of fact, if you're a speaker and you're on the call, you don't have books. You have educational materials. Educational material is part of your speaking package.

So I want to thank everybody for being on the call. I really appreciate it. It was so much fun that I'd probably going to be doing a couple more. I was only planning to do this one.

So I want to thank everybody for being here. My name is Joy Farrington. You could find me on my website at litdiva.com, and I'll talk to you soon. Have a good day. Bye.

End of Transcript

SOURCES FOR STATISTICS

The American Booksellers Association

http://news.bookweb.org

American Demographics

http://www.Demographics.com

American Statistical Association

http://www.amstat.org

The Book Industry Study Group

http://www.bisg.org/
Bowker's Bookwire

http://www.BookWire.com

http://www.BooksInPrint.com

Bureau of Justice Statistics

http://www.ojp.usdoj.gov/bjs/

Bureau of Labor Statistics

http://www.bls.gov/home.htm

Bureau of Transportation Statistics

http://www.bts.gov/

Cap Ventures

http://www.capv.com CIA Factbook download

https://www.cia.gov/library/publications/the-world-factbook/index.html

Cowles/SIMBA Information
http://www.simbanet.com Euromonitor International http://www.euromonitor.com/ FedStats http://www.fedstats.gov/ Gallup Organization http://www.Gallup.com IDEAlliance, Inc. http://idealliance.org

An independent, nonpartisan resource on trends in American public opinion.

http://www.pollingreport.com/ Information Technology Industry Council http://www.itic.org

National Center for Education Statistics
Outsell Inc.

http://www.outsellinc.com   Polling   Report
http://www.pollingreport.com State & County
QuickFacts http://quickfacts.census.gov/qfd/
Statistics.com http://www.statistics.com
Statistics on the Web
http://www.execpc.com/~helberg/statistics.ht
ml Subtext/open Book Publishing
http://www.subtext.net
Transaction   Publishers
http://www.transactionpub.com UK Statistics
http://www.statistics.gov.uk/default.asp
United Nations Statistics
http://www.un.org/Depts/unsd
United States Department of Commerce, U.S.
Census Bureau. http://www.census.gov/
US Census Bureau http://www.census.gov

World statistics—Read Stats in Real Time
http://www.worldometers.info

WRITERS RESOURCES
Social Media Tools
Teleconference
FreeConferenceCall
InstantTeleseminar
FreeConferenceCalling
Rondee
FreeConferencePro
Google Voice

Webinars
Instantteleseminar

Podcast/Online Radio
Cinch.fm
BlogTalk Radio
TalkShoe

Create an Online Course
Creating an online class or e-course is a great way to distribute your work, expand your following and create an additional stream of income

Platforms for Creating an E-Course/Online Course

Elearning- Turn your existing material into an online system

Udemy- Take and Create Online Course

E-Learning Zoom- Create an Interactive Learning Experience

Flextraining: LMS Learning Software

Content Development

OER Commons- Offers free content for e-courses

The Online Book Page- Find Free Books for Your E-Course

CCAC Online Learning- Offers tips for streamlining Media into your E-course

Federal Resource for Educational Excellence- Name says it all

Biz/ed: Offers Content with a focus on Business

TopMarks: Offer Content on a Wide Range of Topics

Open CourseWare Consortium: Opensource E-courses you can incorporate into your Online Course

Product Fulfillment
Vervante
Kunaki.

Create an Online Magazine
Scoopit

Paper.li
Yudu
Publishing Platforms
eBooks
Barnes and Noble-Pubit!
Kindle- KDP Program
Vook
Smashwords

Print on Demand
CreateSpace
Lulu
Lightning Source
Organize Your Team and Business
Zoho
BackPack
White Board: Create, Edit, and Share a document
Campfire: Create a private Chat-room that you can use like Instant Messaging. Includes
Conference Calls Upgrade
GroupMe: Group Messengering that Works with Skype
Wiggio

Miscellaneous Tools
The Alphabetizer: Paste your list into the text box, and the site will alphabetize it for you

Absolute Write
http://absolutewrite.com/
AutoCrit-Editing **Software**
http://www.autocrit.com/
The Digital Reader
http://www.the-digital-reader.com/
Legal **Writes** **Publication**
http://legalwritepublications.com/
The **Freelance** **Writers** **Den**
http://freelancewritersden.com/
Project **Gutenberg**
http://www.gutenberg.org/wiki/Main_Page
The **Purdue** **Online** **Writing** **Lab**
http://owl.english.purdue.edu/
Writers Café
http://www.writerscafe.org/
Writing.com
http://writing.com
Writers Digest
http://writersdigest.com

BIBLIOGRAPHY

(n.d.). Retrieved September 9, 2012, from Dictionary.com: http://dictionary.reference.com/browse/niche

(n.d.). Retrieved September 9, 2012, from Dictionary.com: http://dictionary.reference.com/browse/blurb? s=t Plessinger, A. (n.d.).

. Retrieved *The Effects* from Vanderbilt *of Mental Image University: on Athletic* http:// www*Performance*.vanderbilt.edu/AnS/psycholo gy/health_psychology/ mentalimagery.html . (2012, August). Retrieved September *Traditional* 9, 2012, *Trumps* from *Vanity* http://www.allclassicbooks.com: http:// www.allclassicbooks.com/why-traditional- publishers -trump-self-publishing

Notes